This coloring book belongs to

AF241616

____

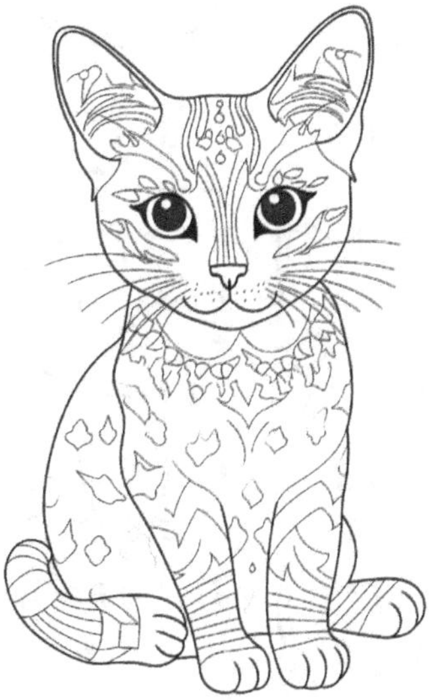

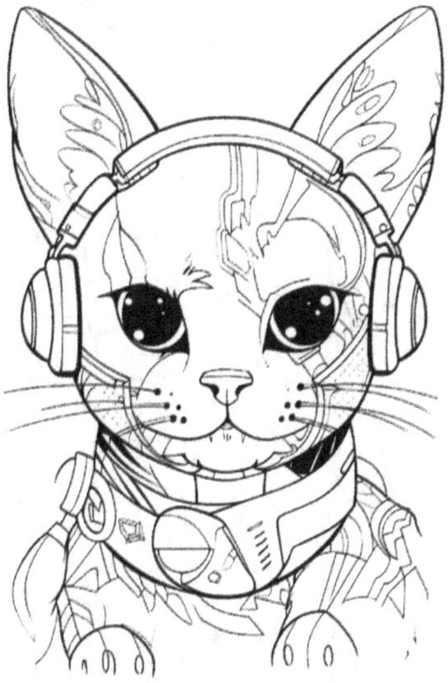

Love this Coloring book?
Want to show off your masterpiece?
Do you want your art displayed on our website?

1. Take a picture of a finished coloring page
2. Scan the QR Code to go to our website
3. Upload the photo of your finished coloring page

OR

Use #happytimesbooks or mention us @happytimesbooks on Instragram to have it displayed on our front page

No registration required

If you are under 18 please get a parents permission

https://happytimesbooks.com/pages/customer-art

Color Test Page

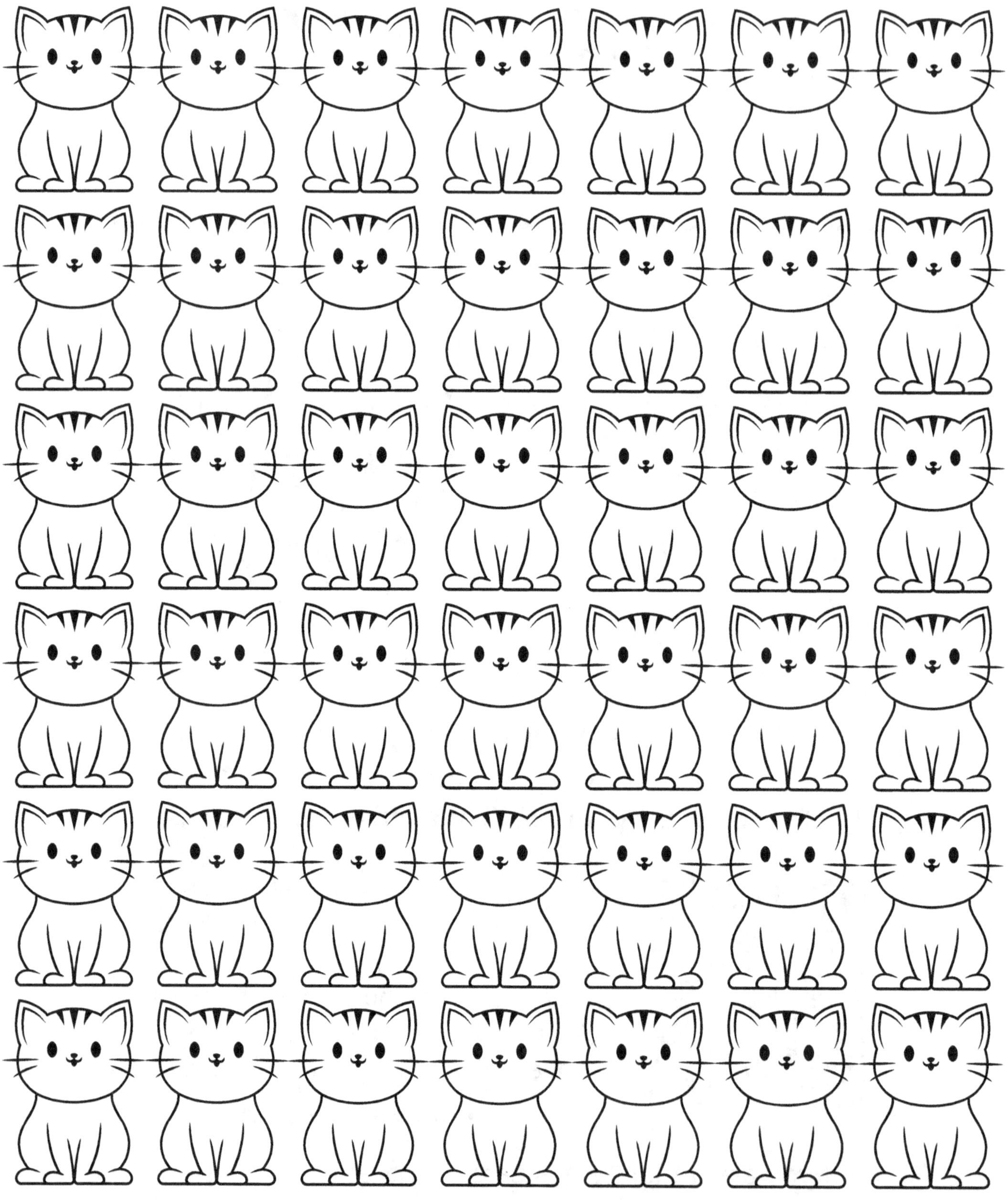

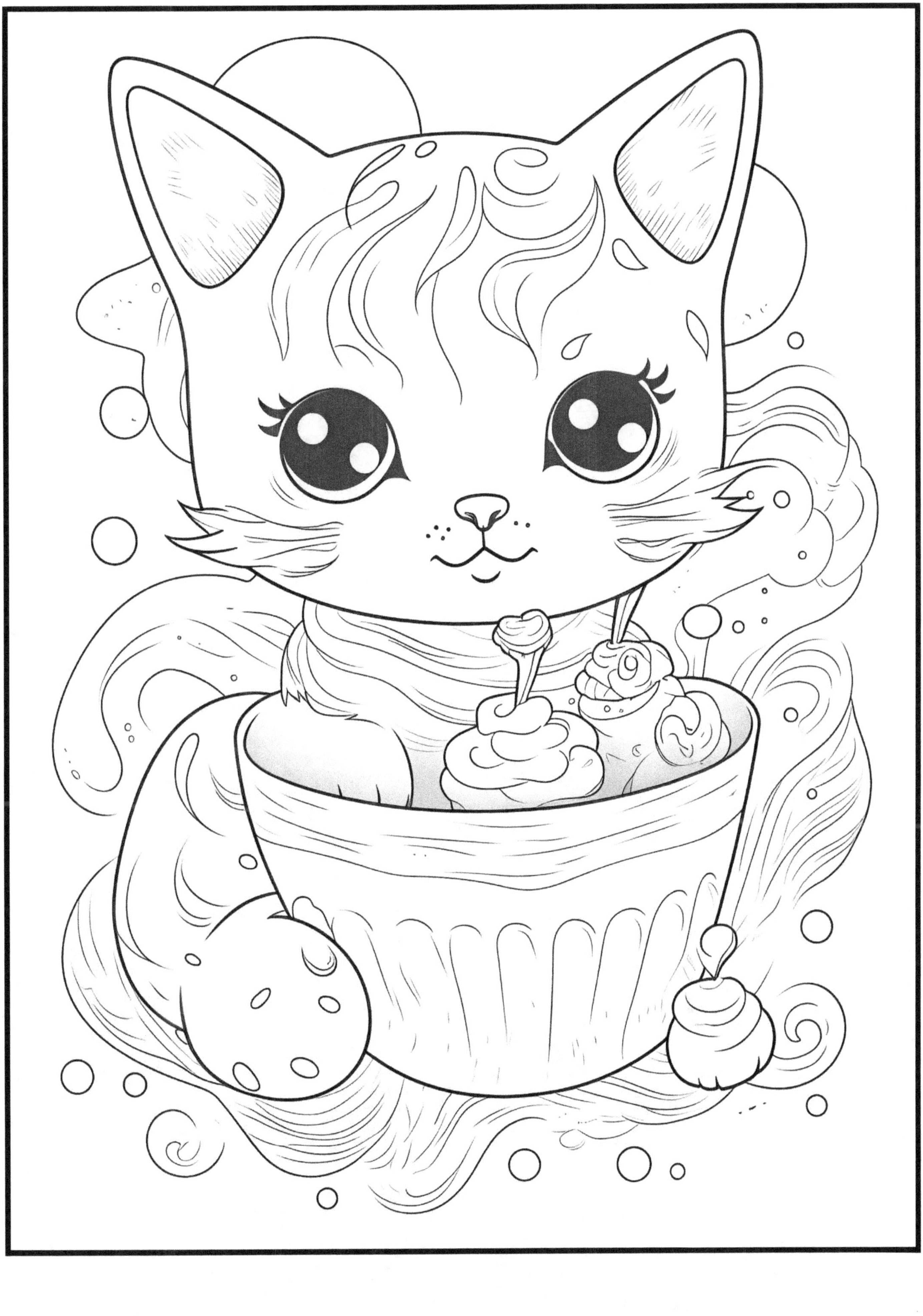

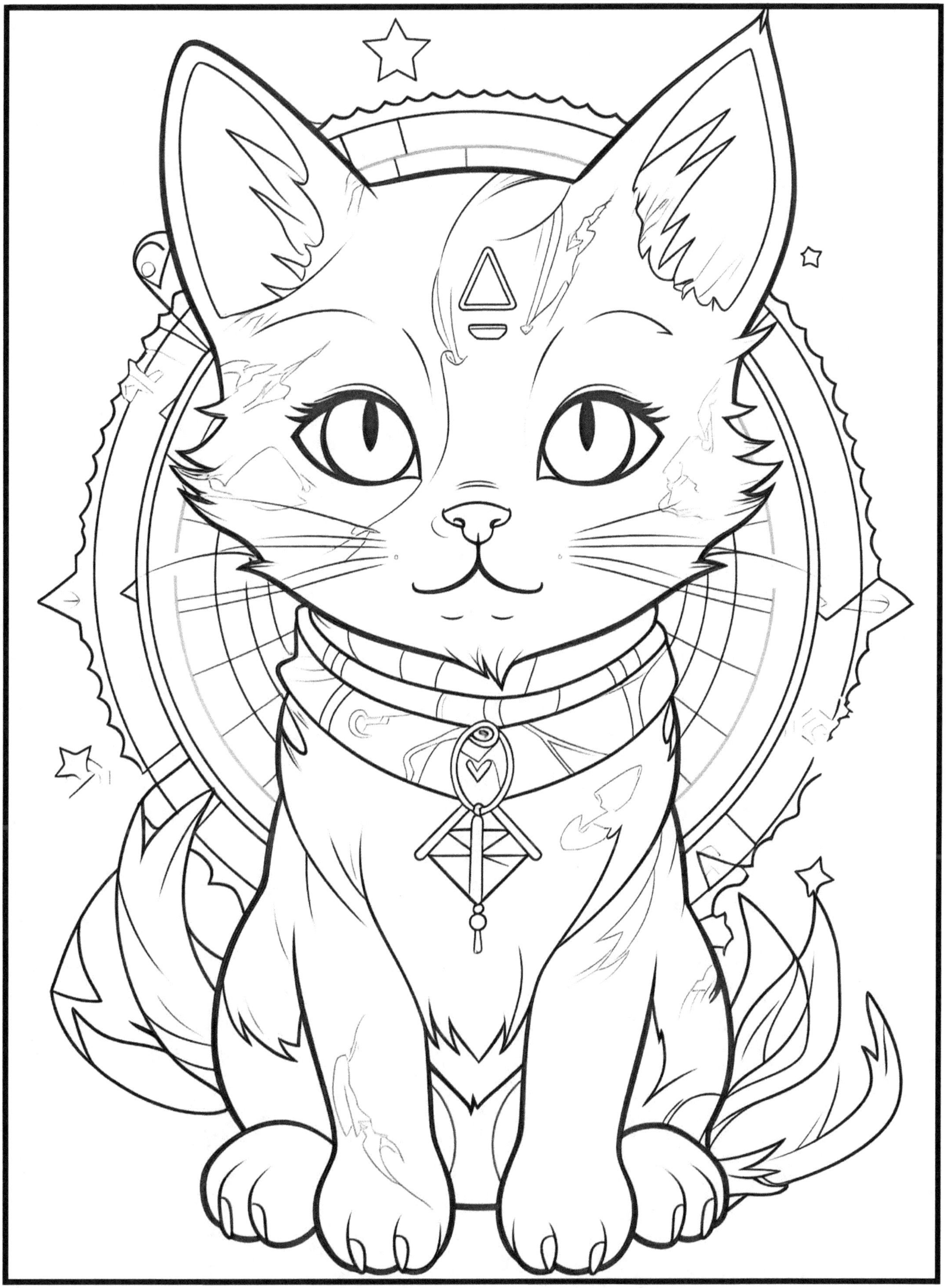

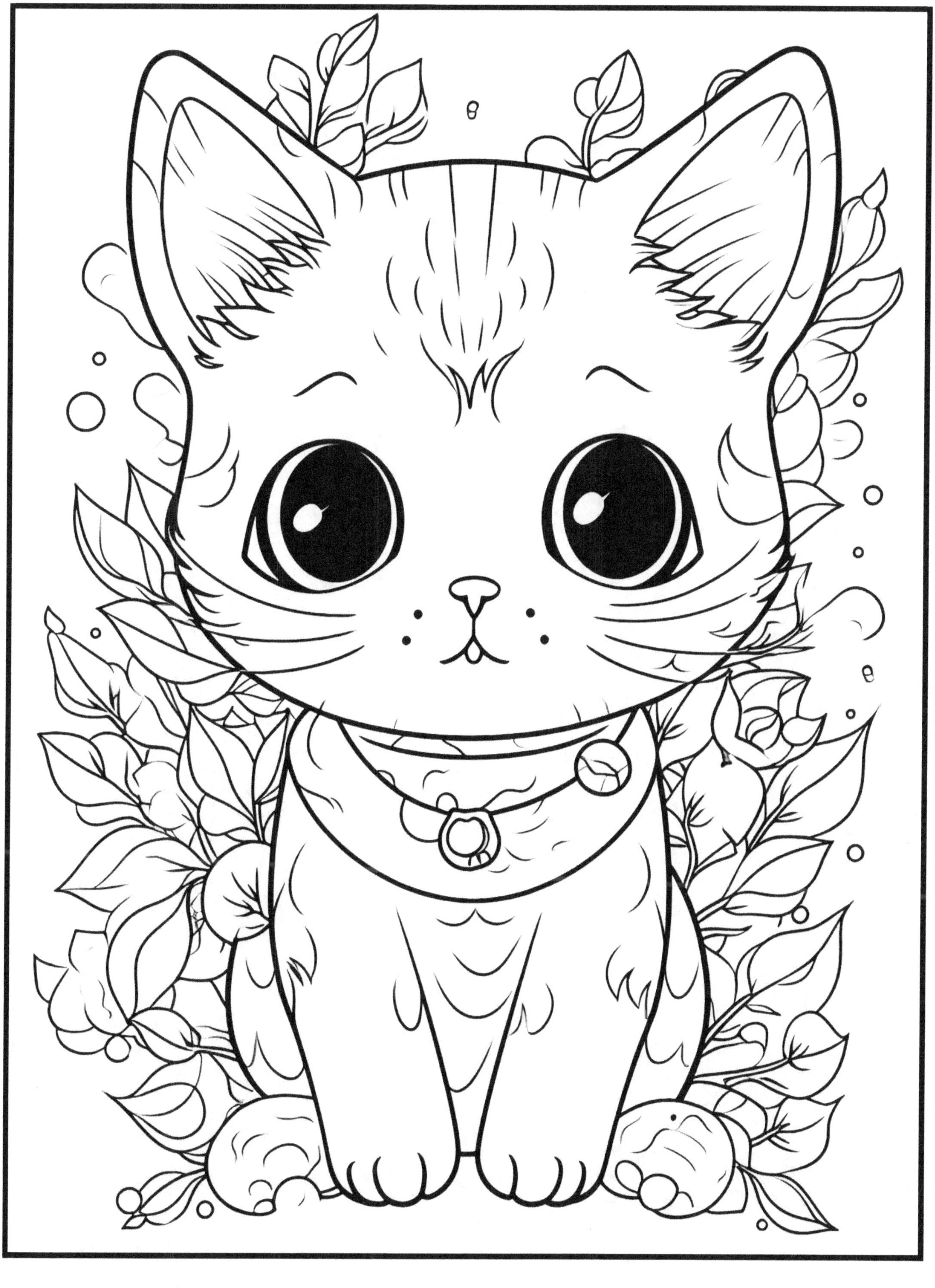

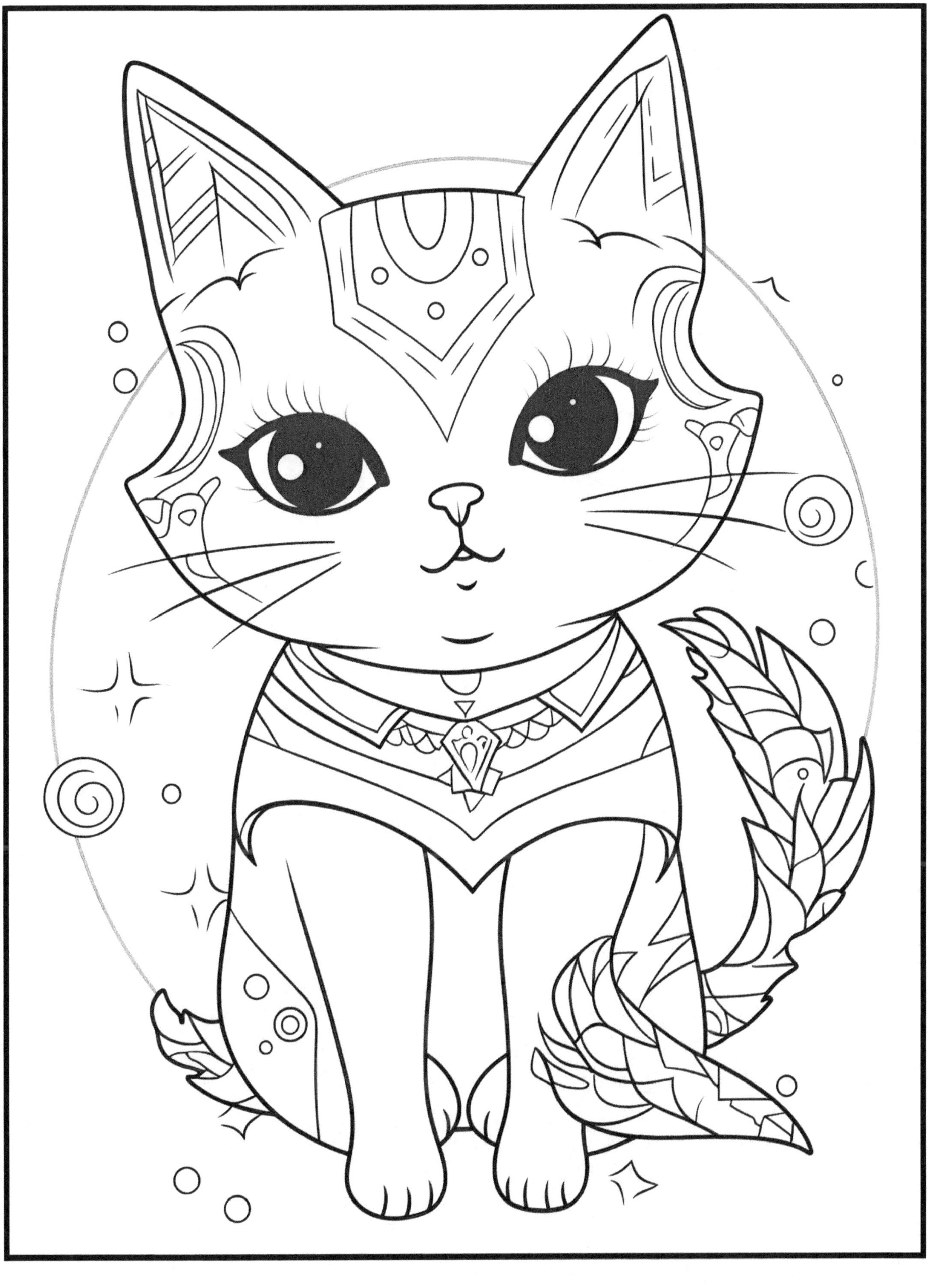

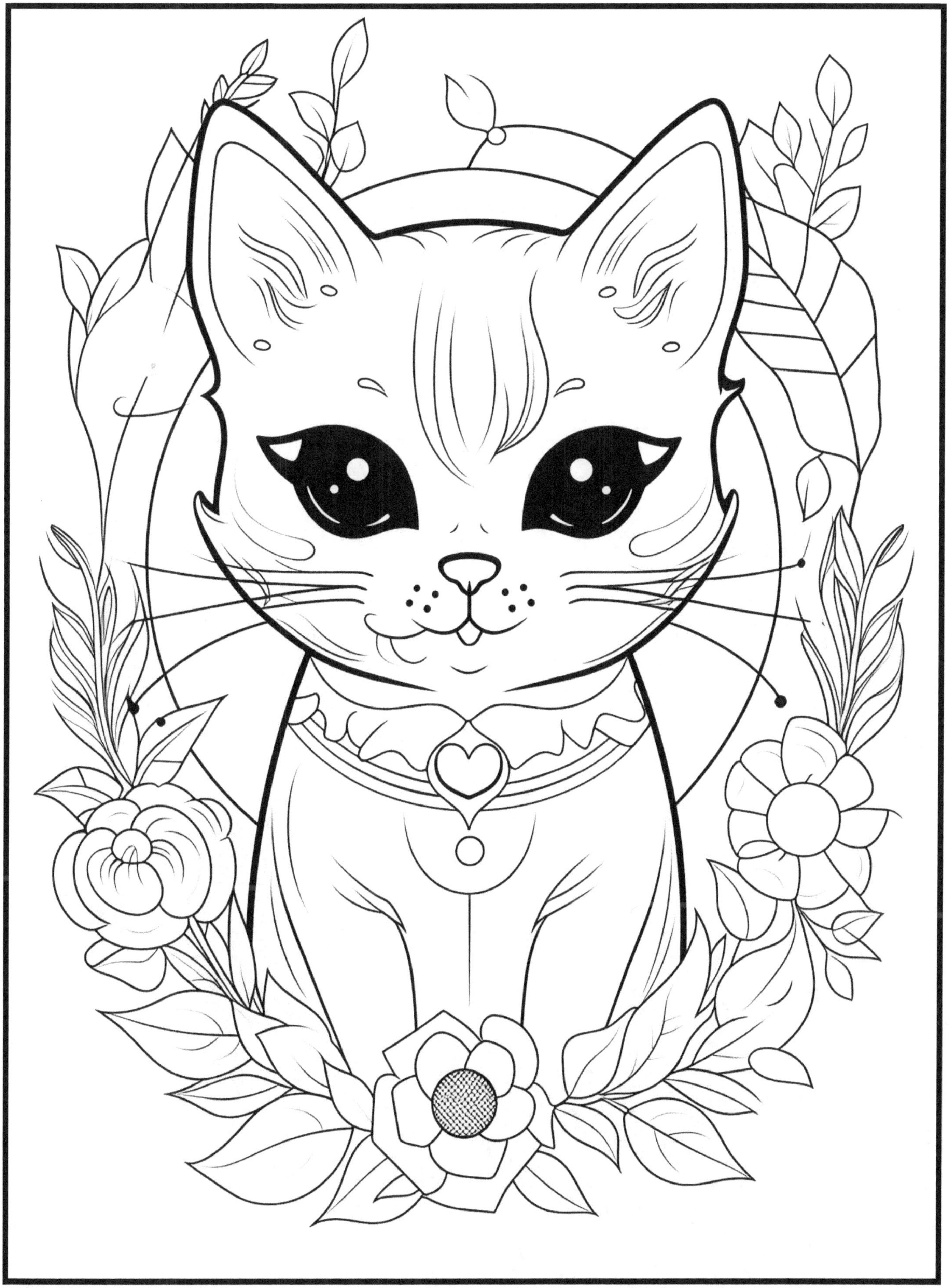

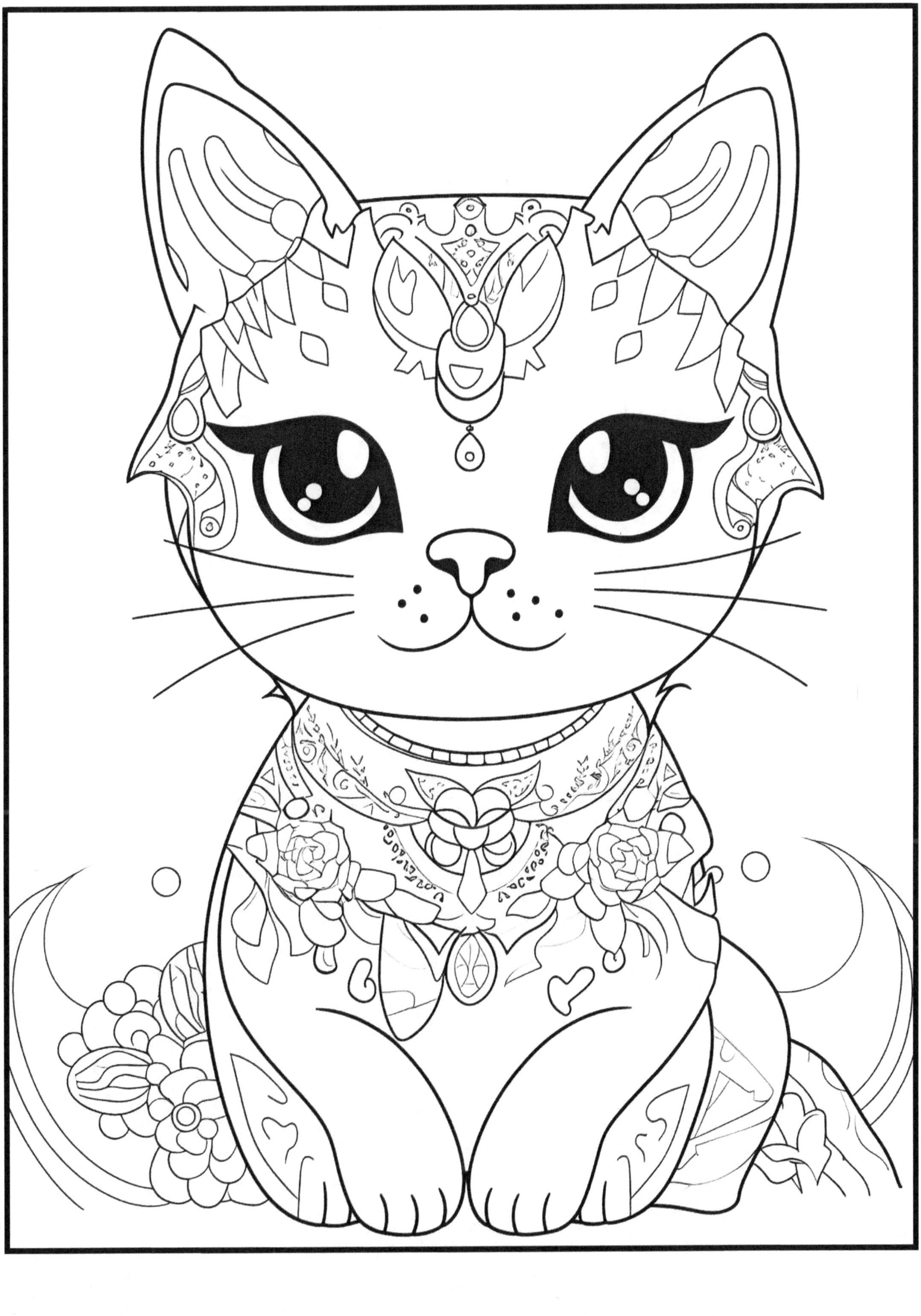

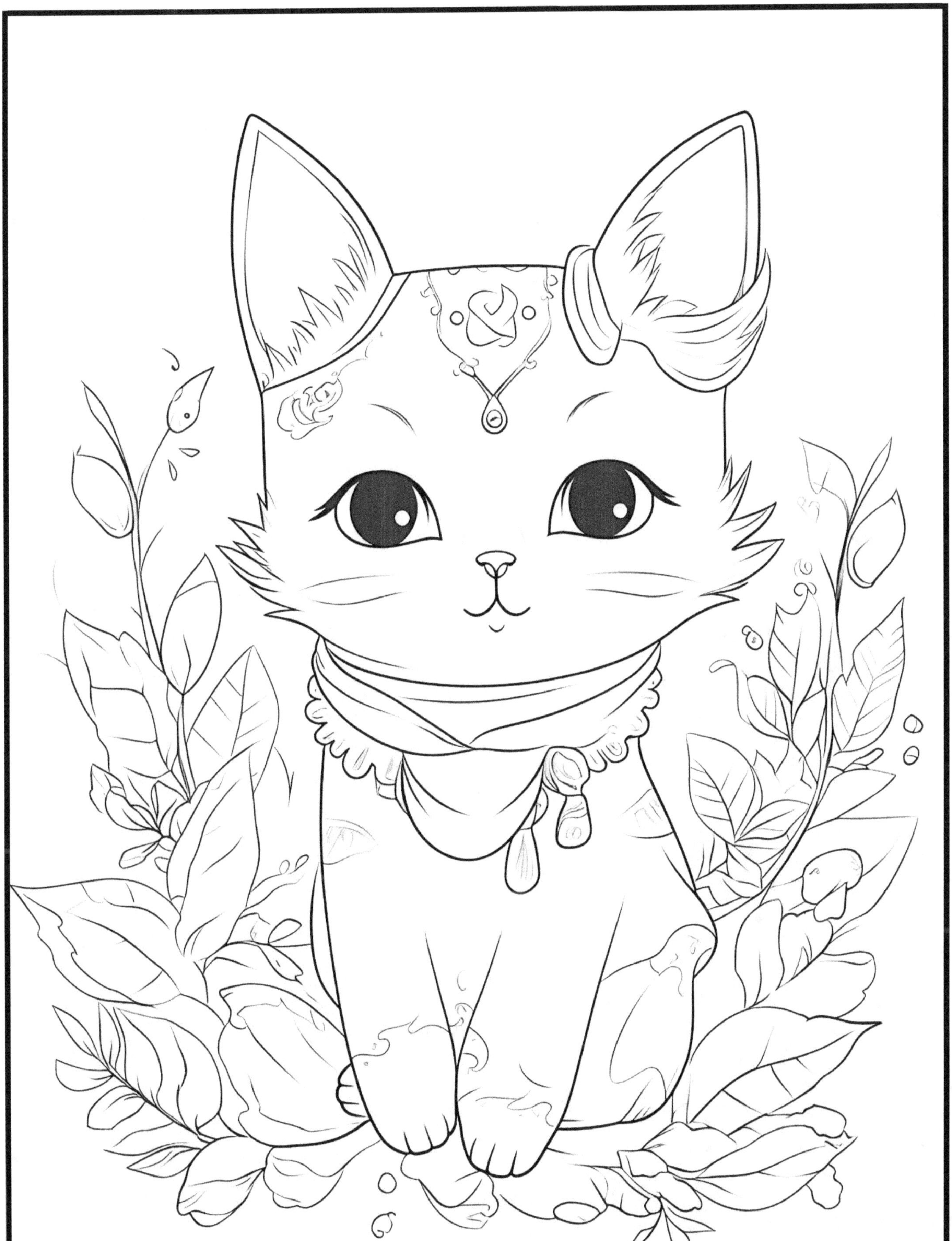

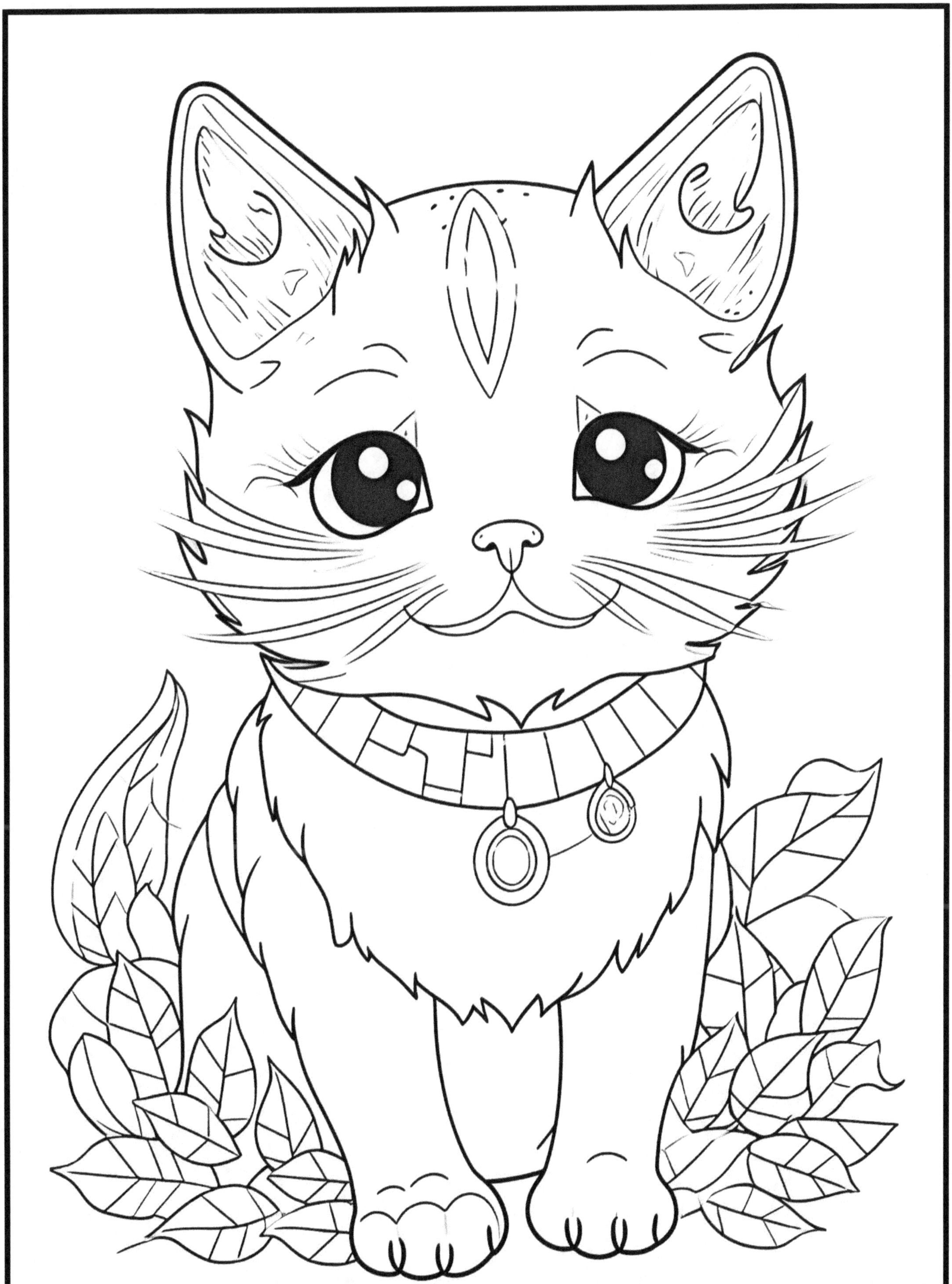

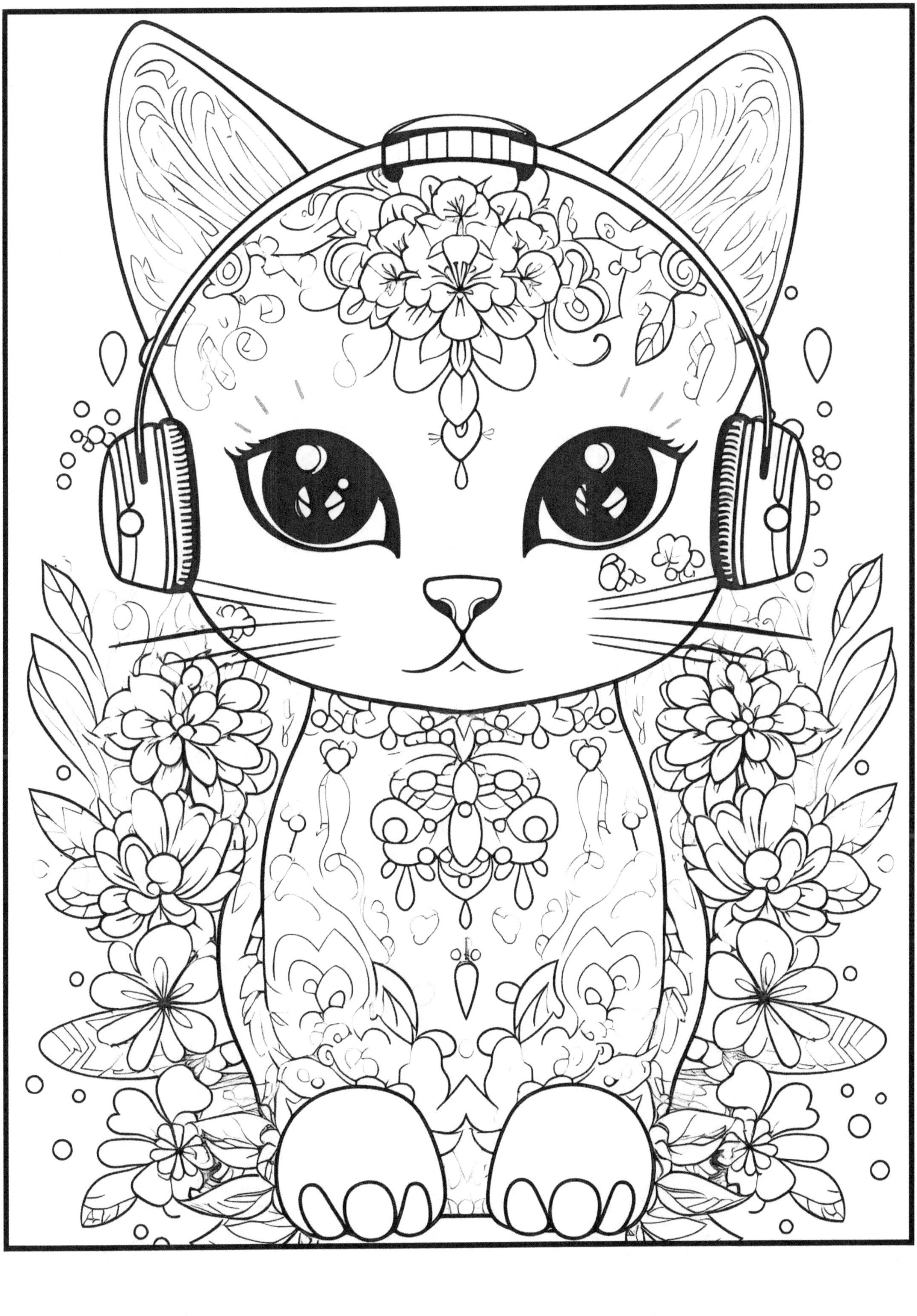

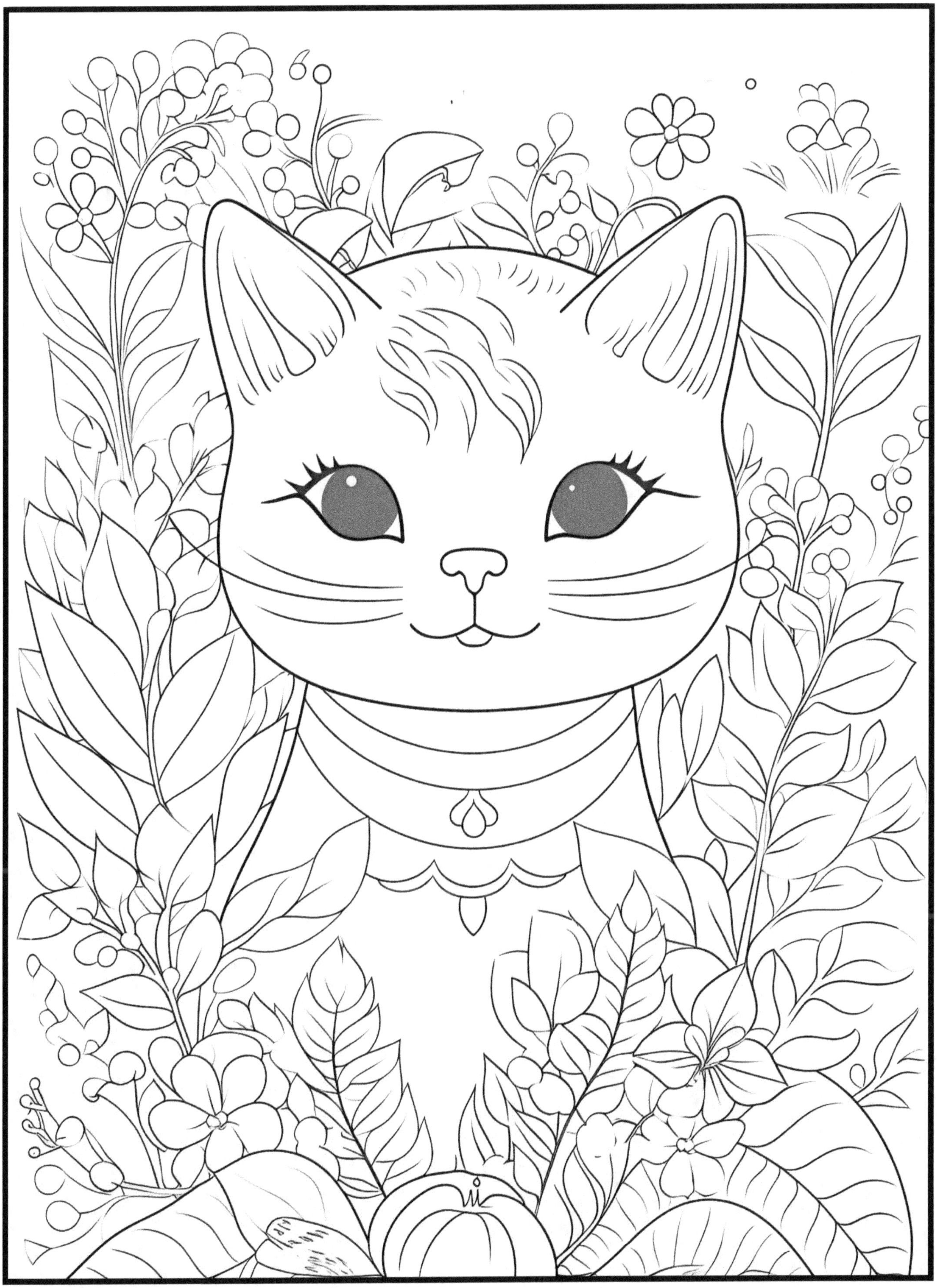

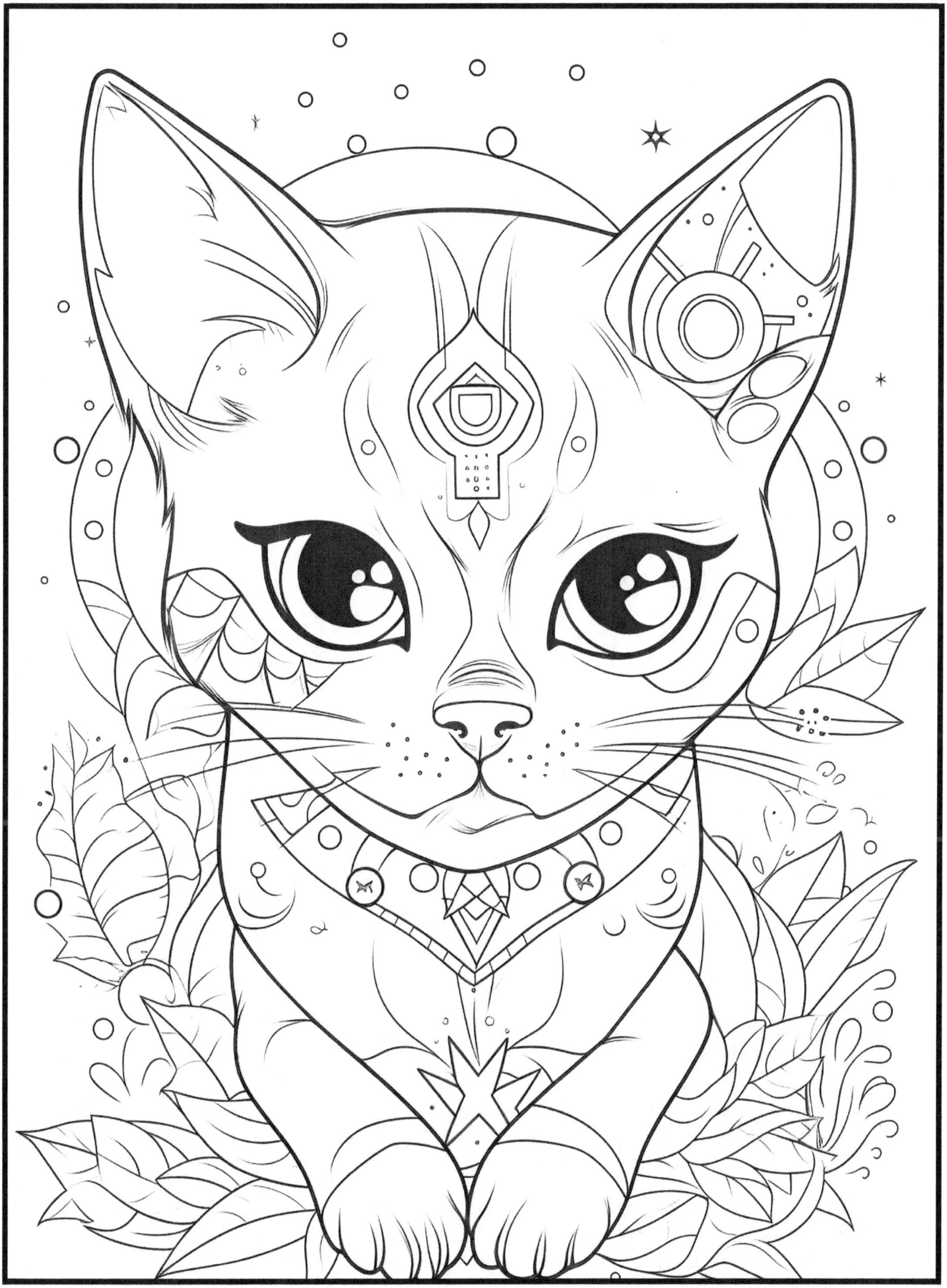

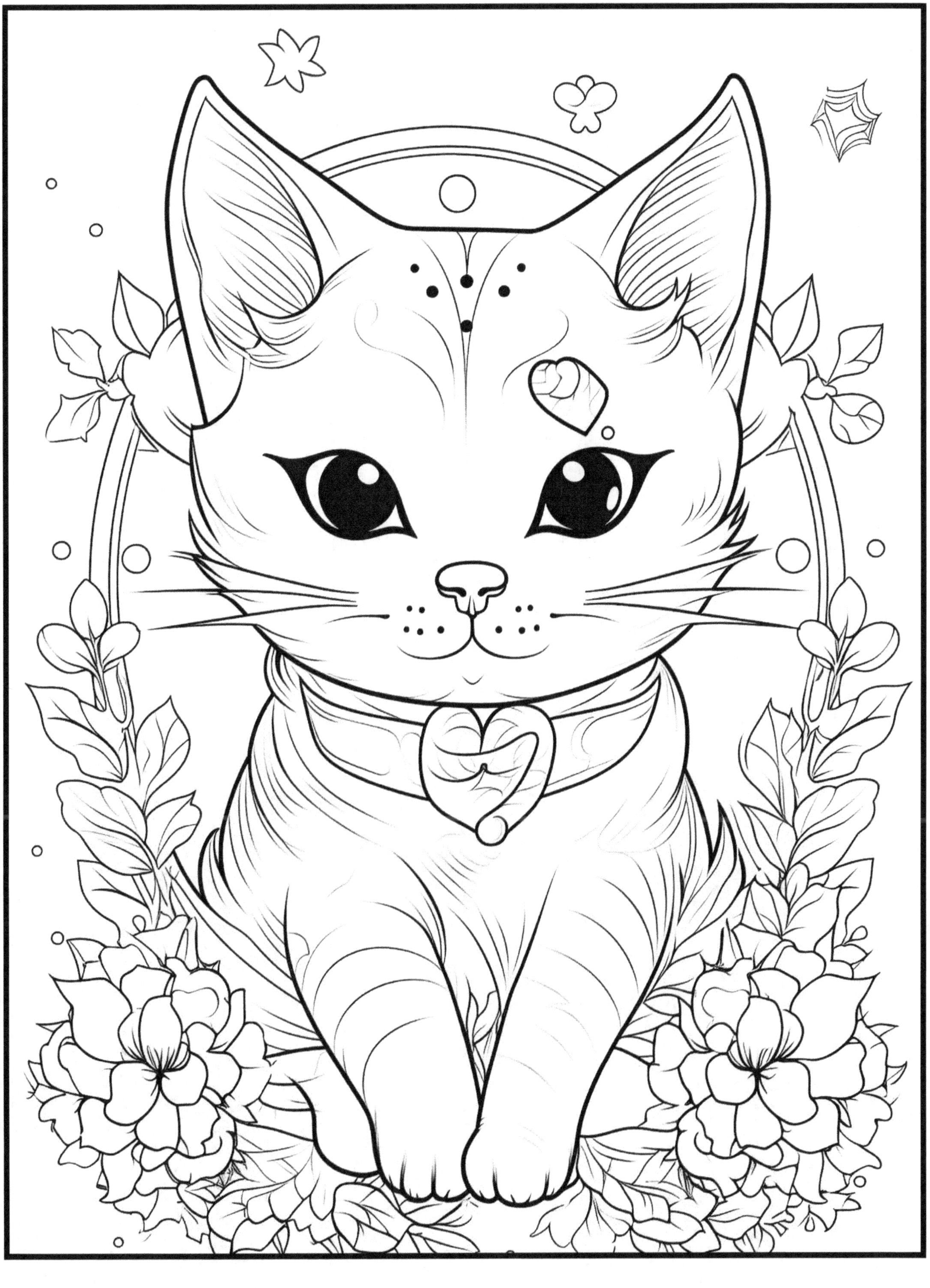

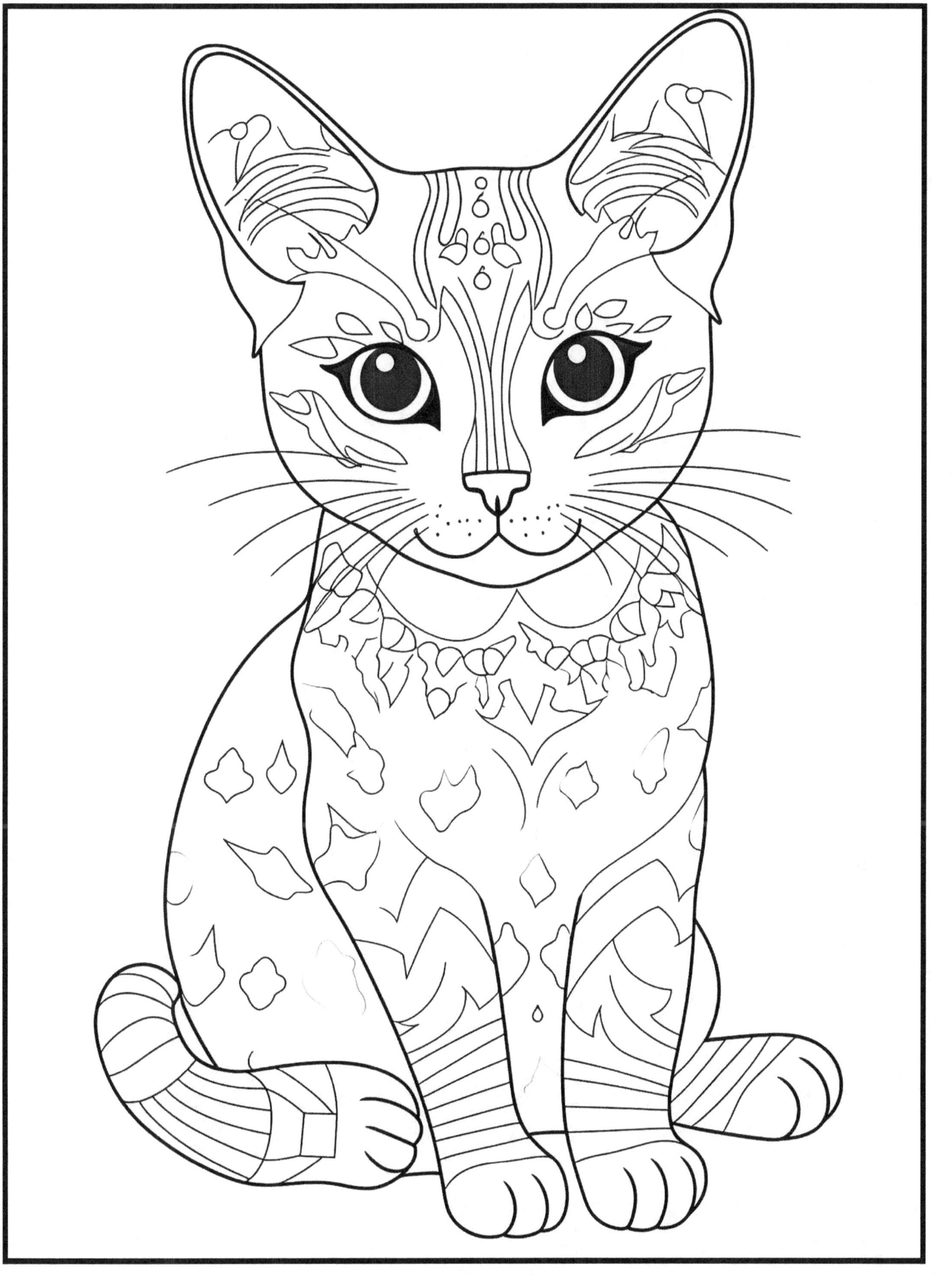

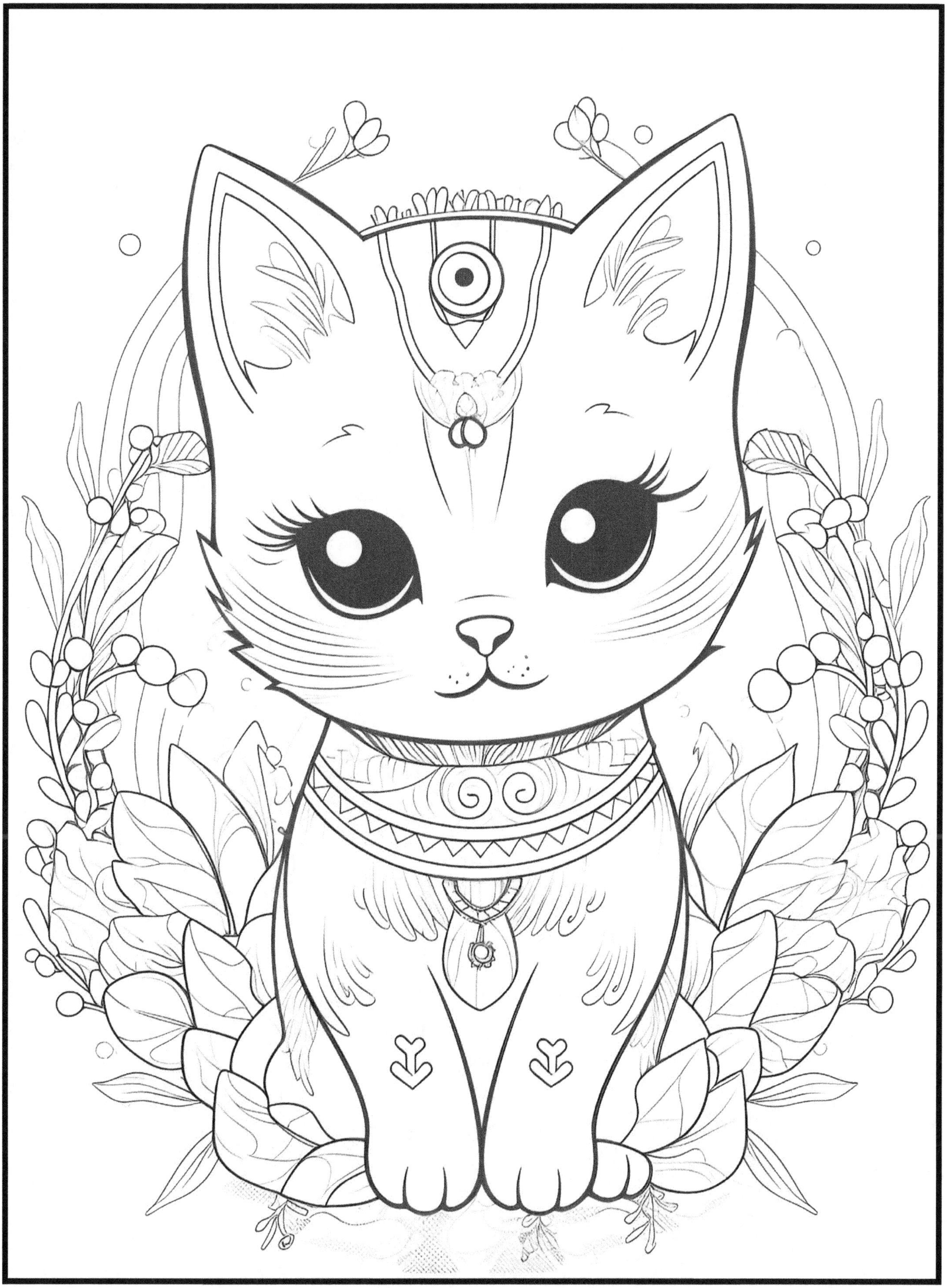

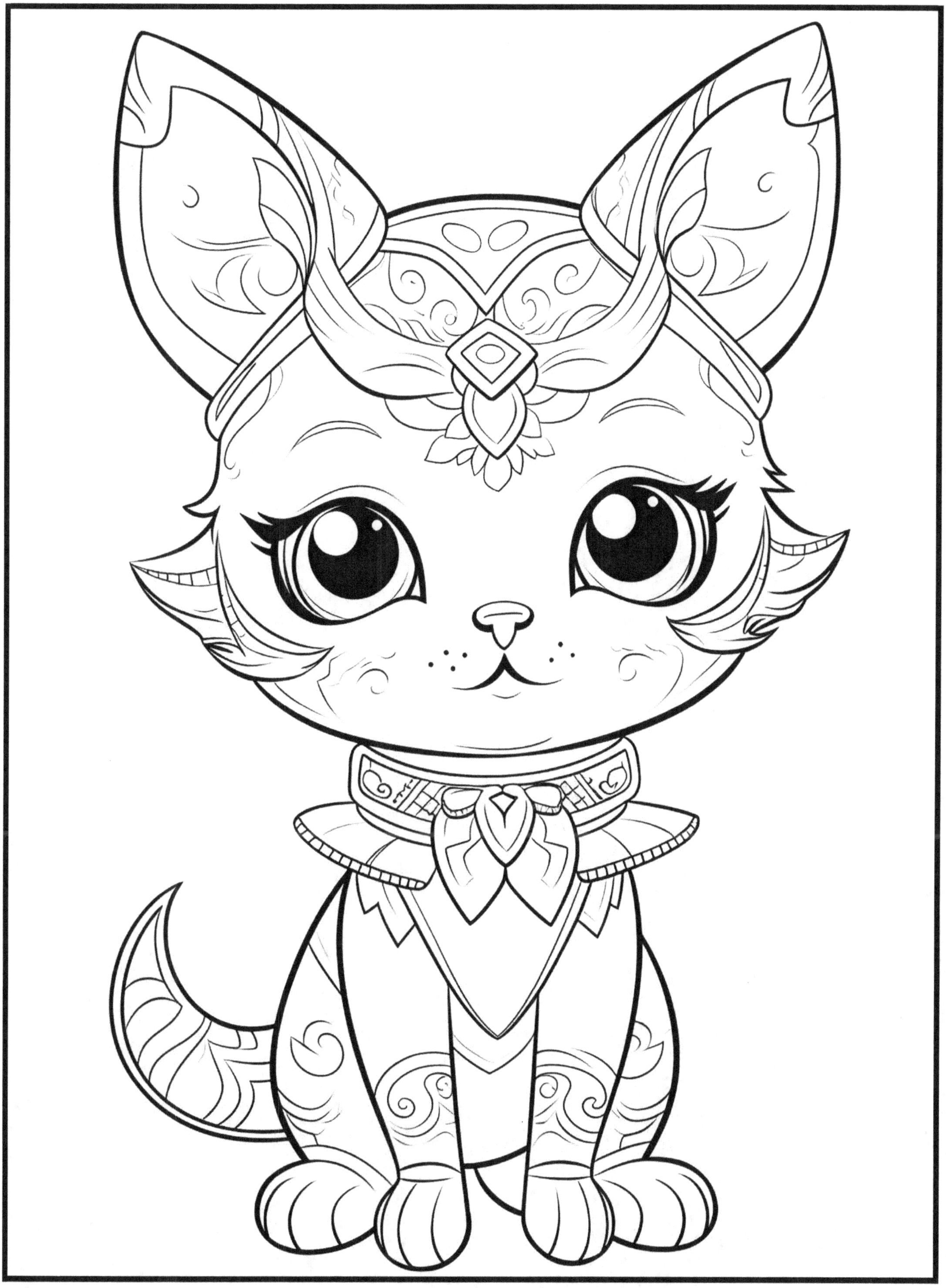

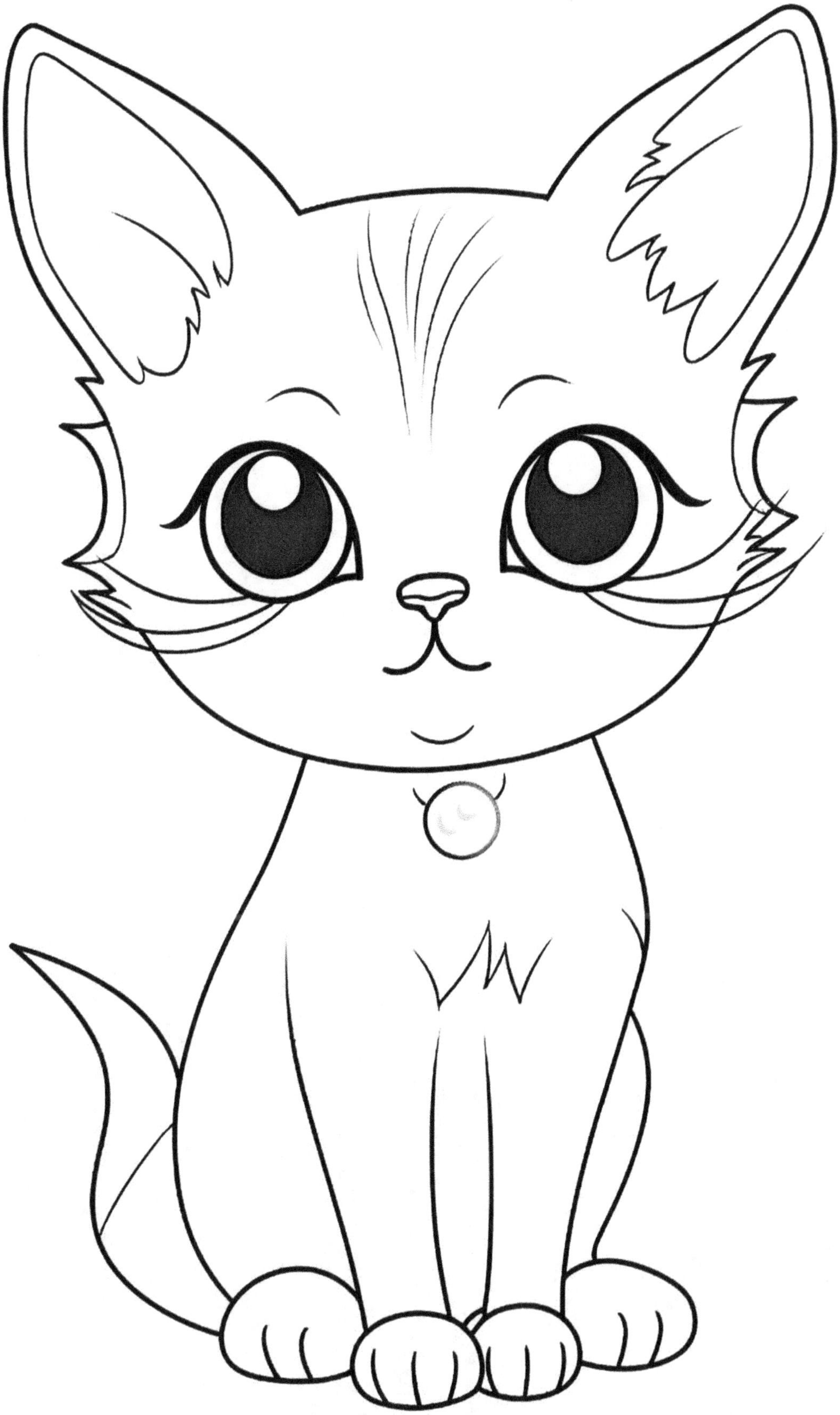

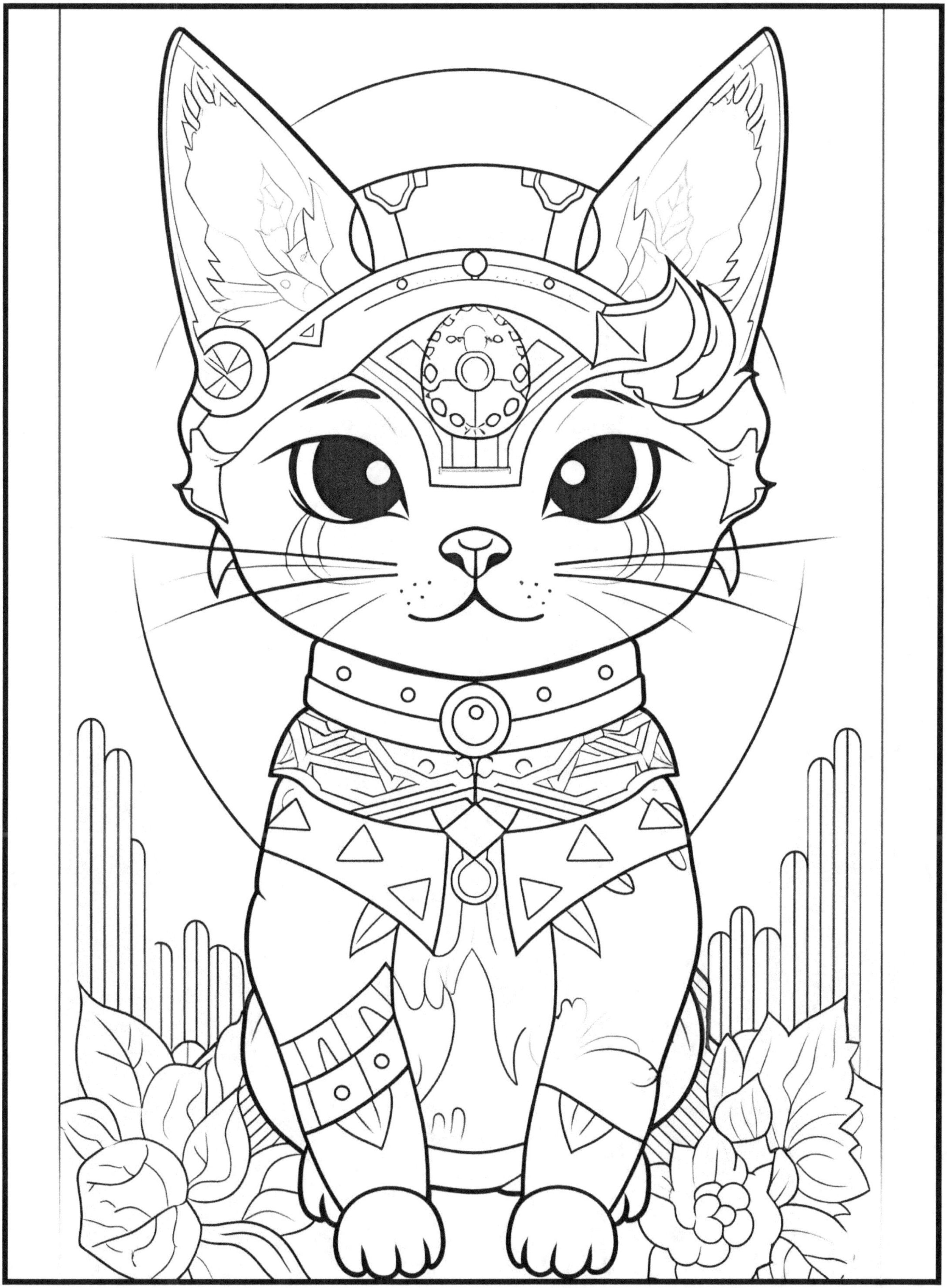

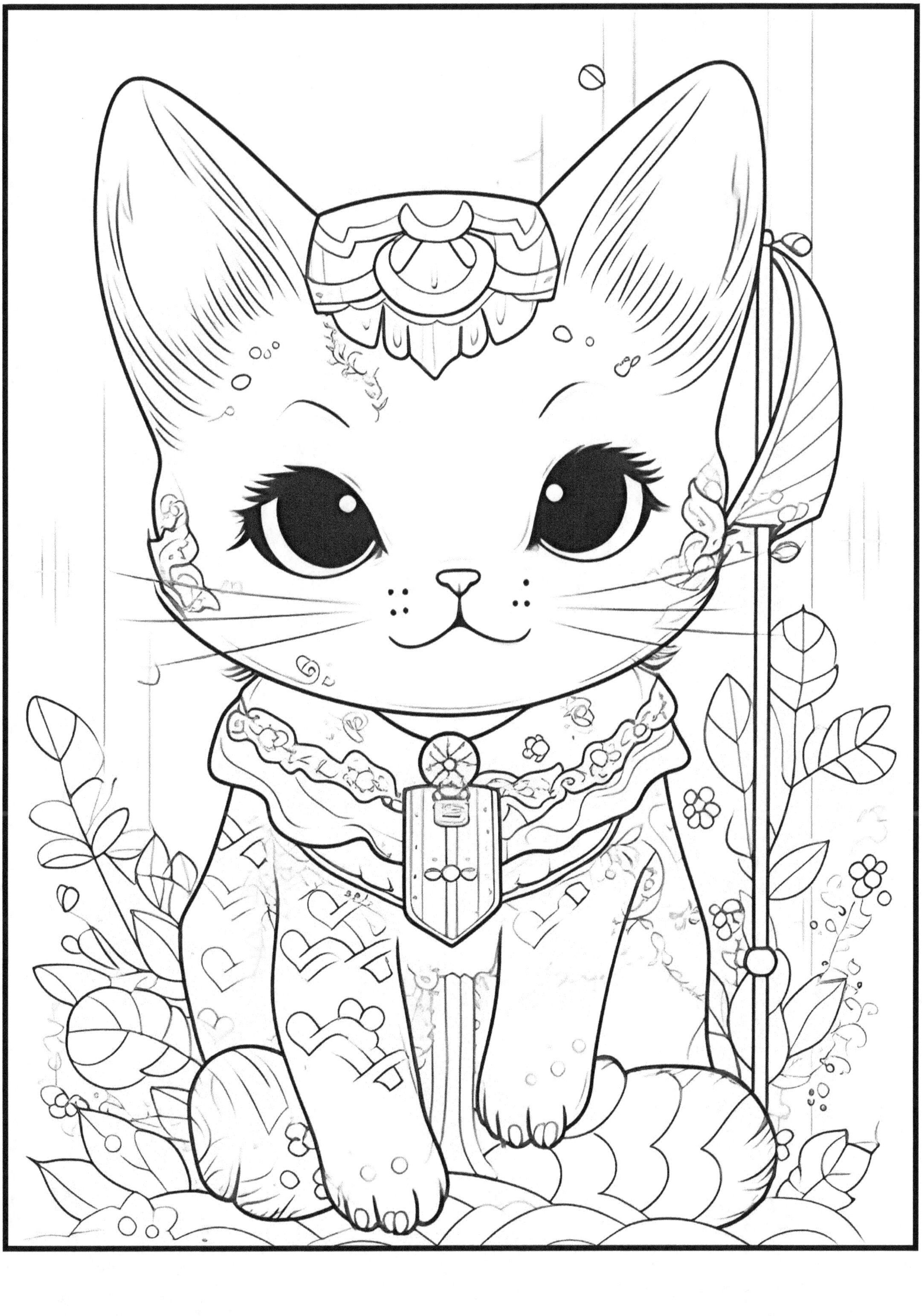

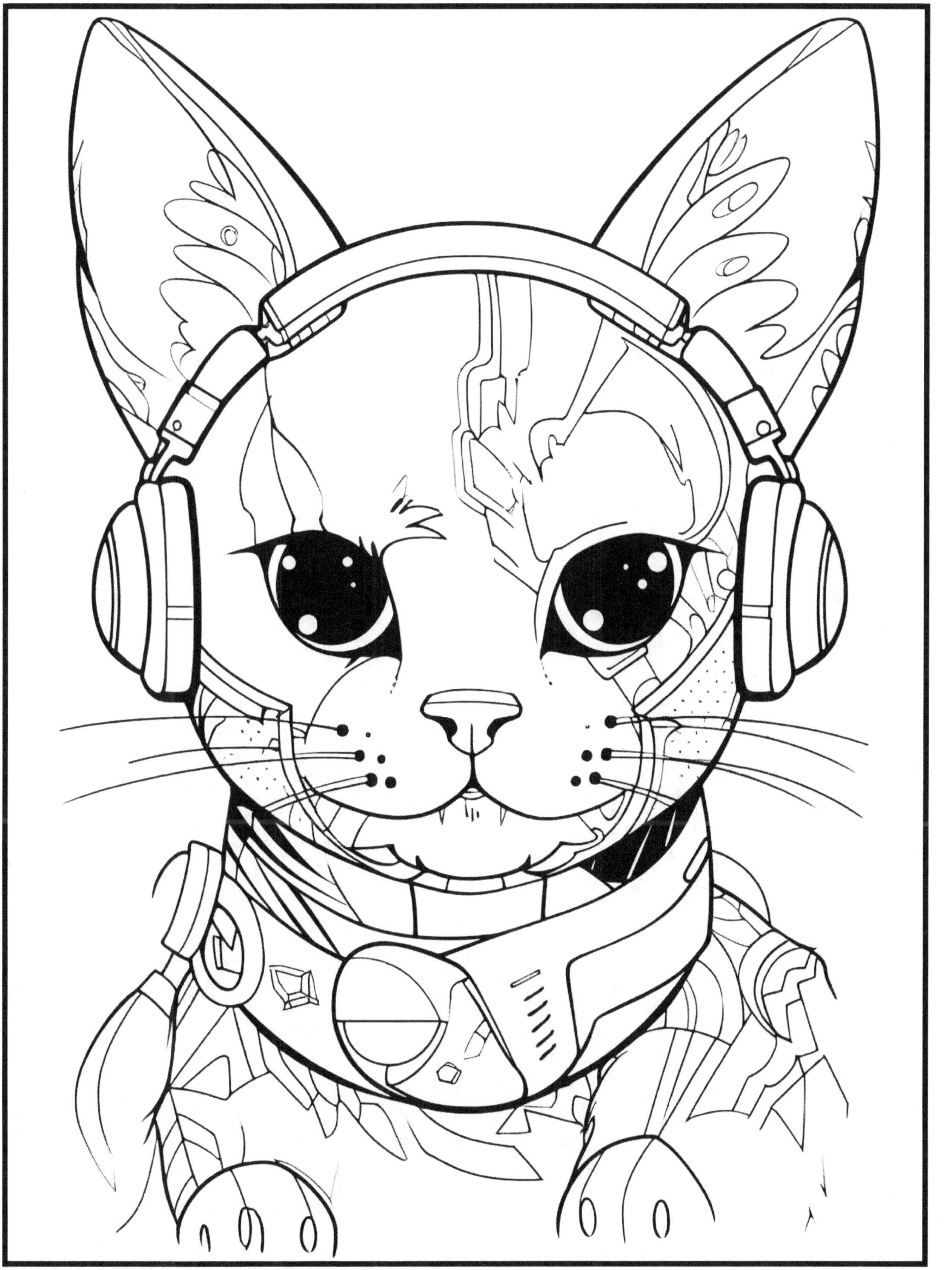

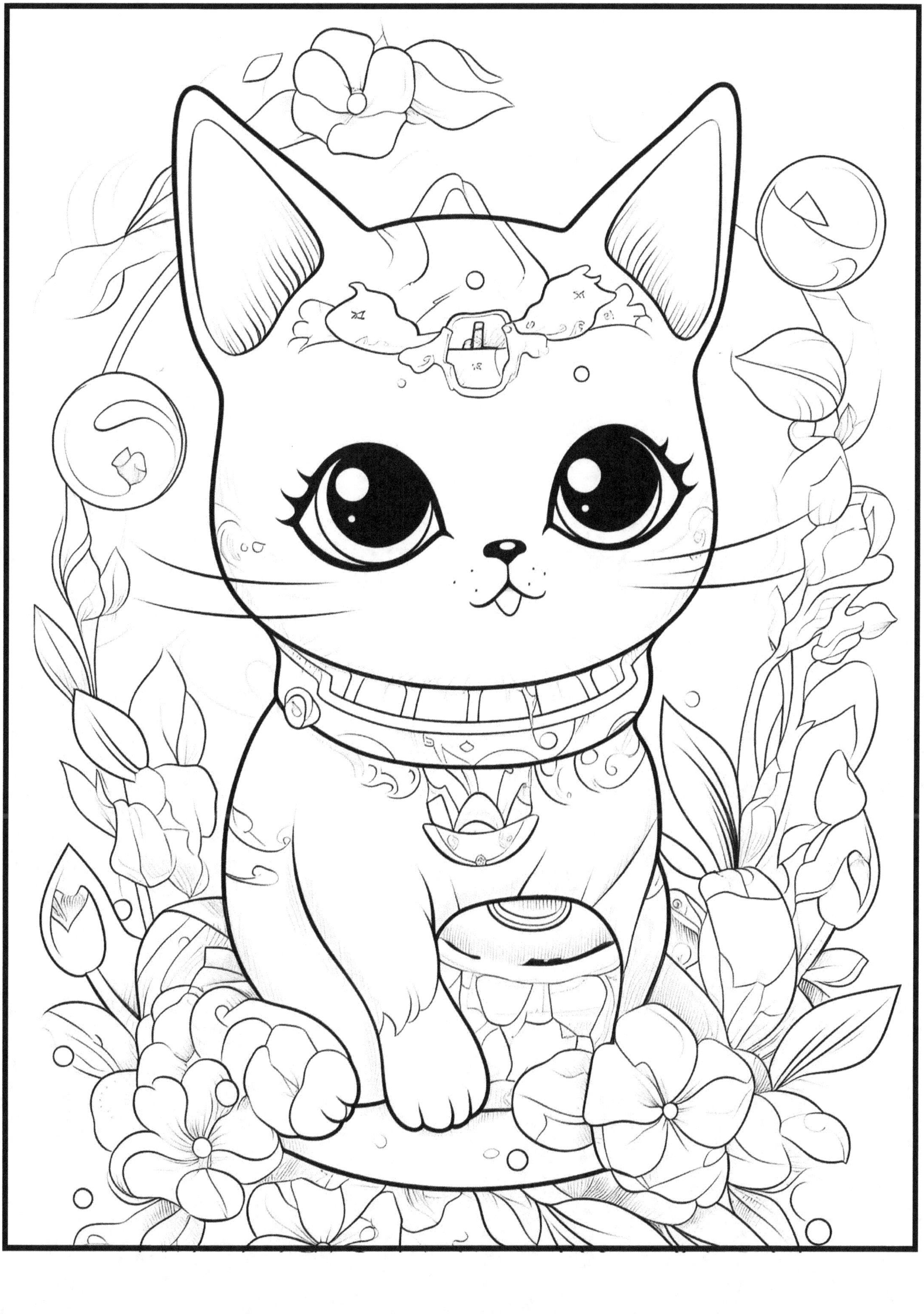

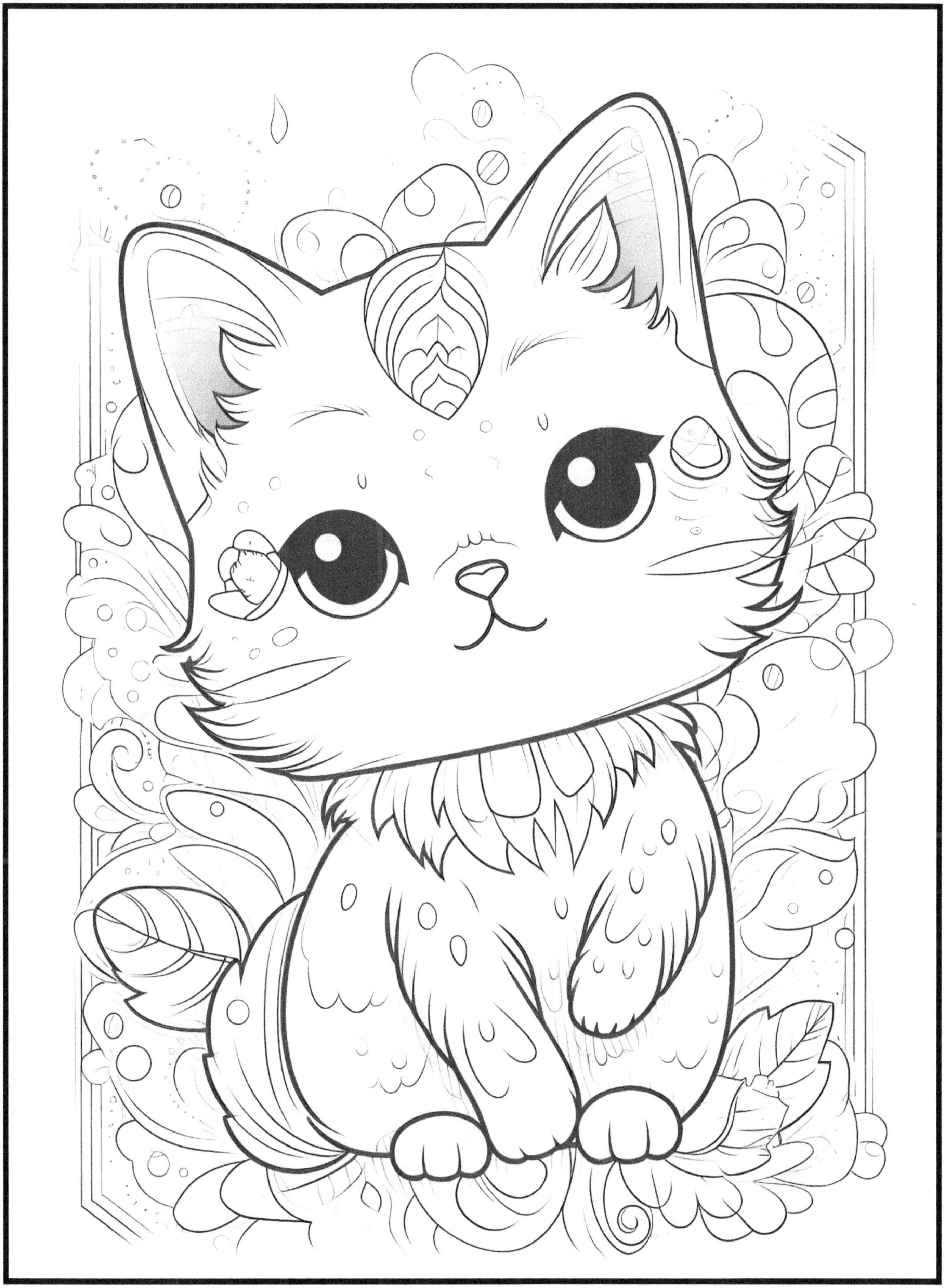

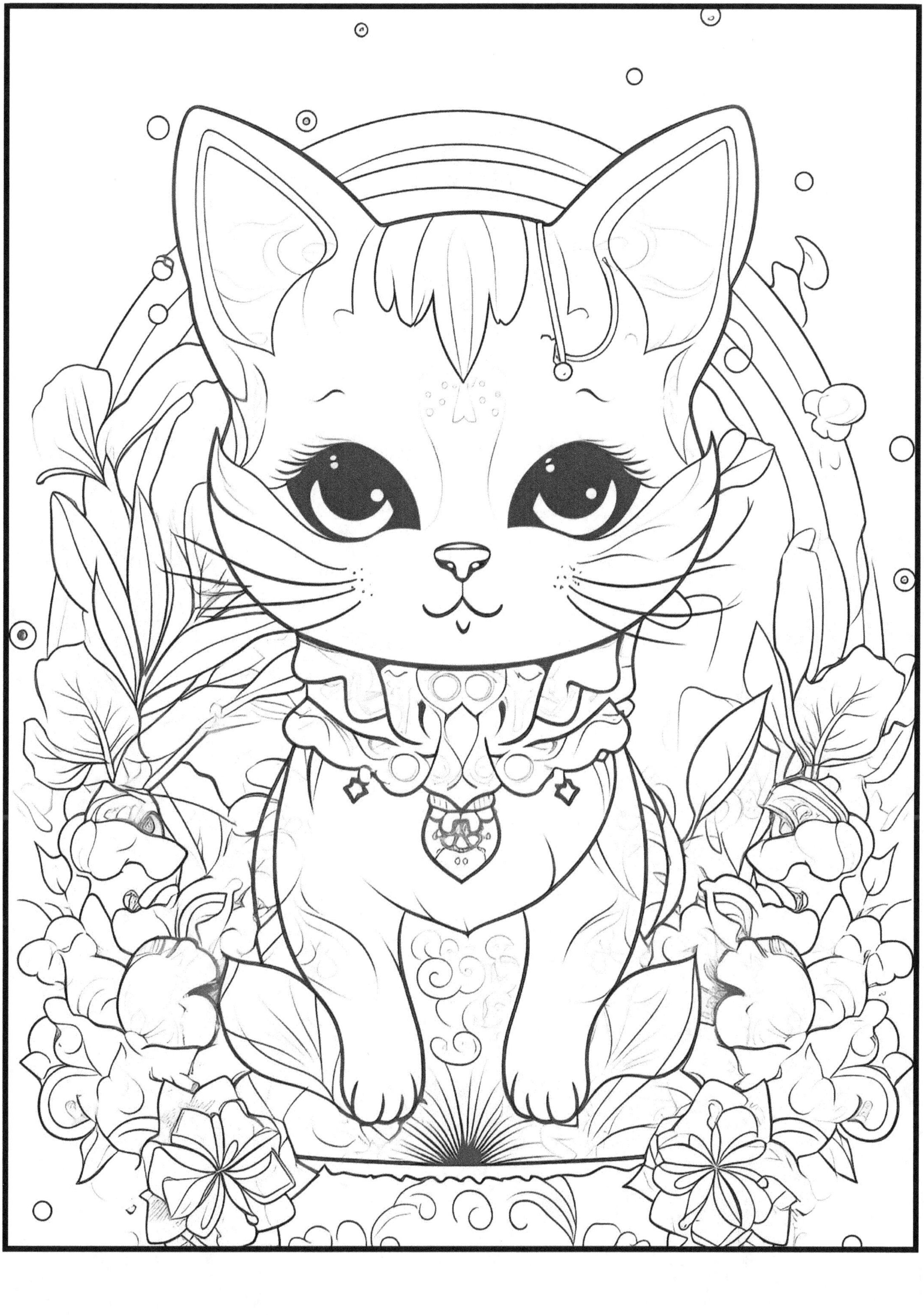

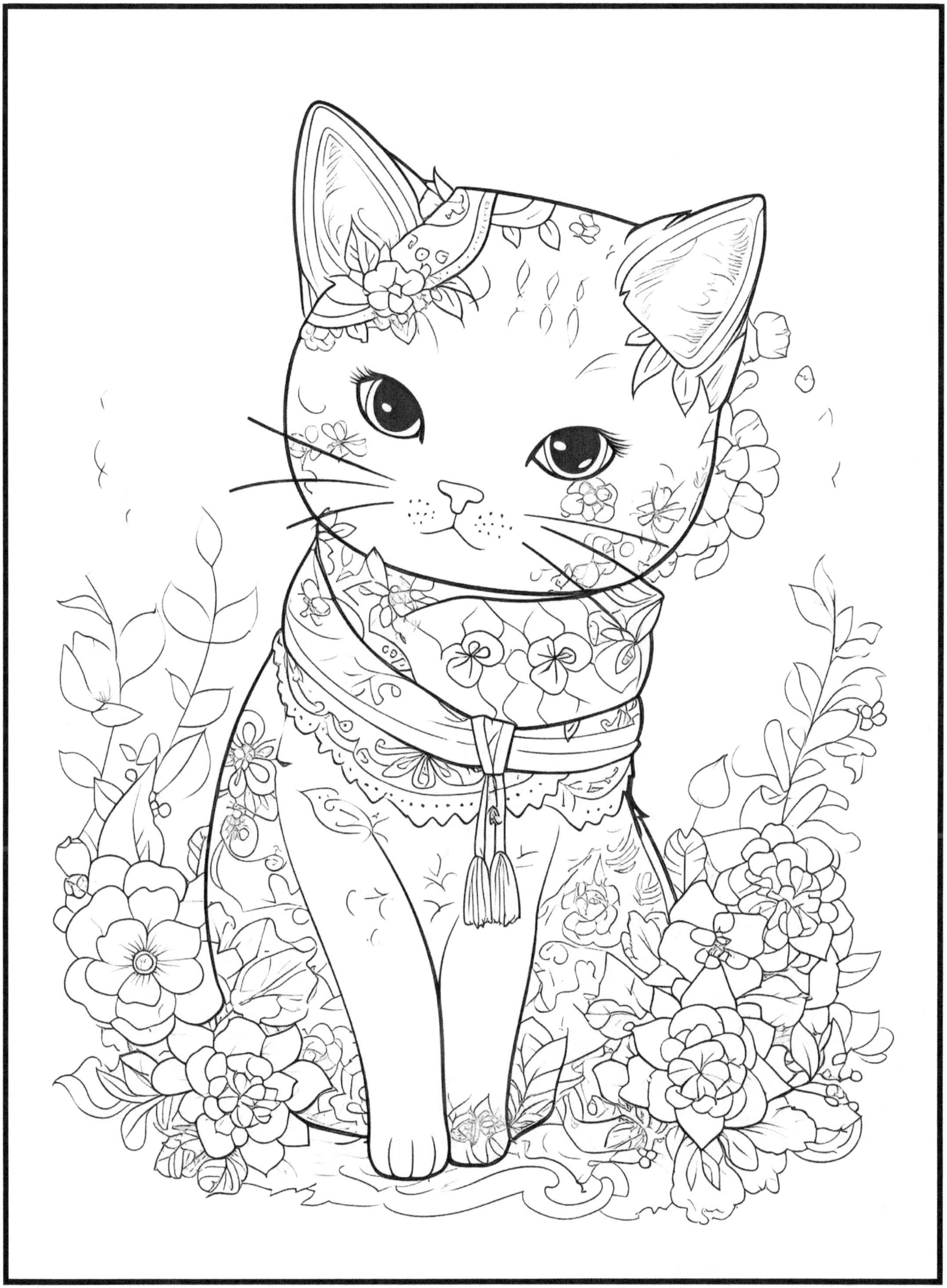

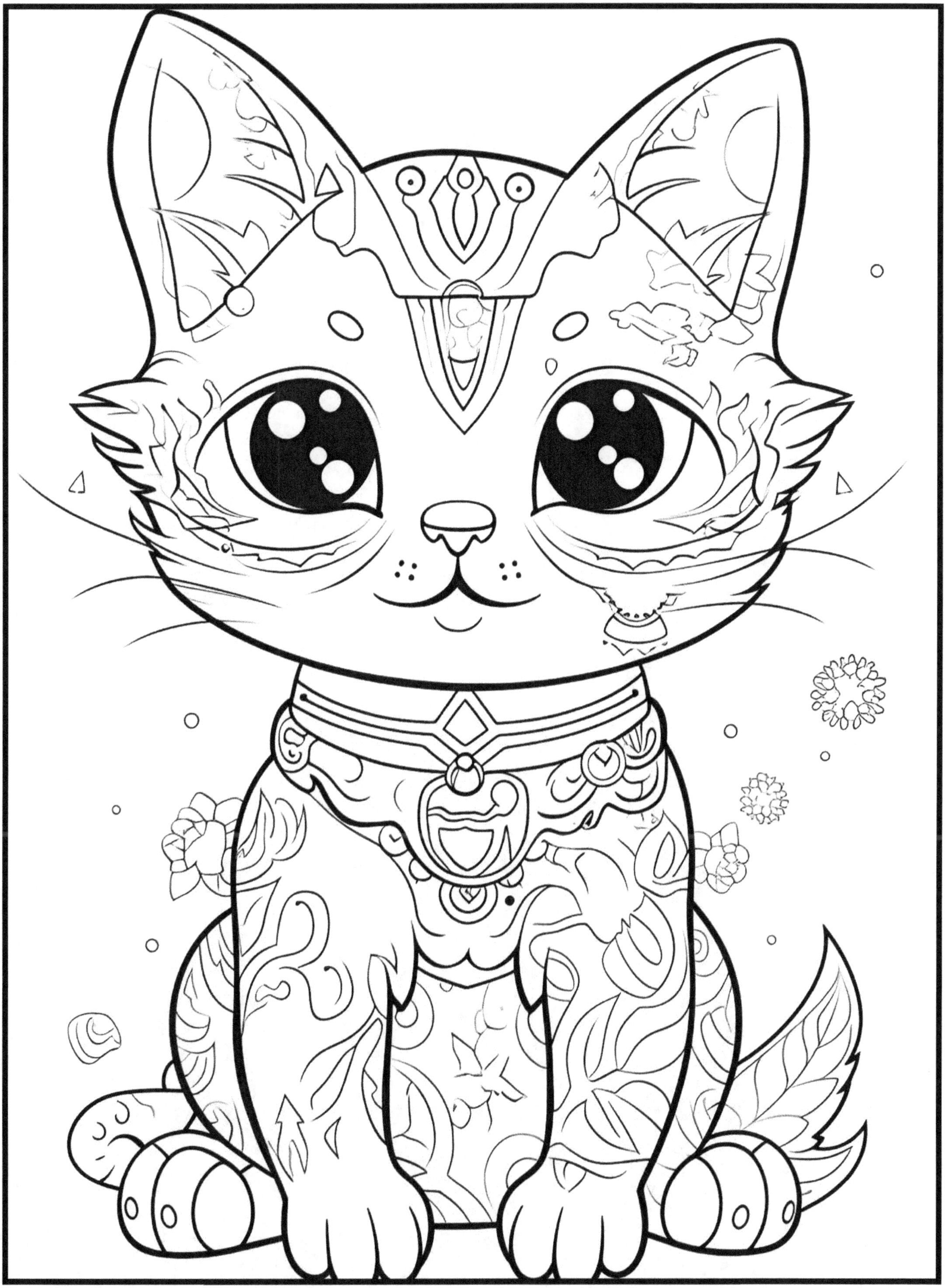

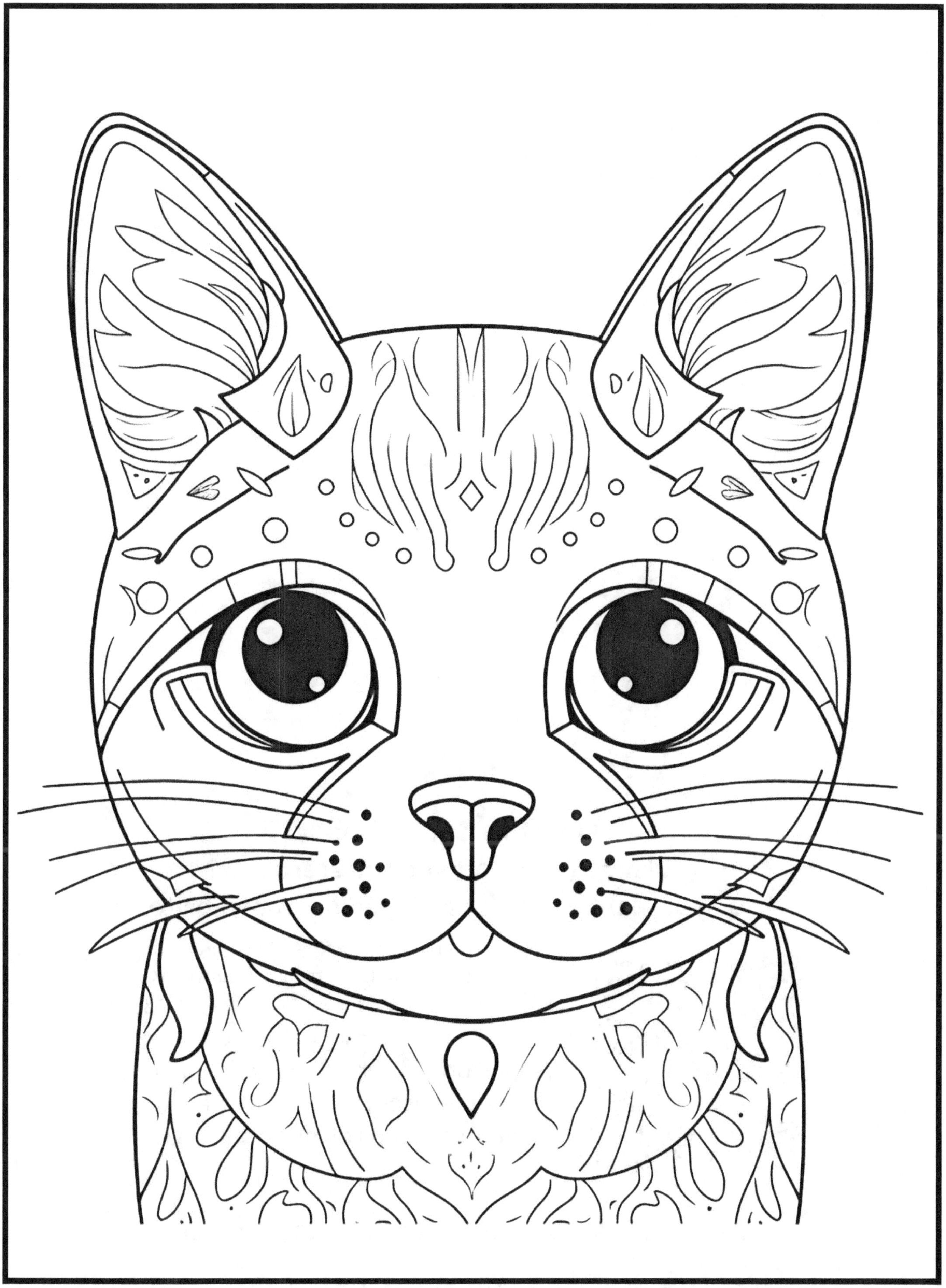

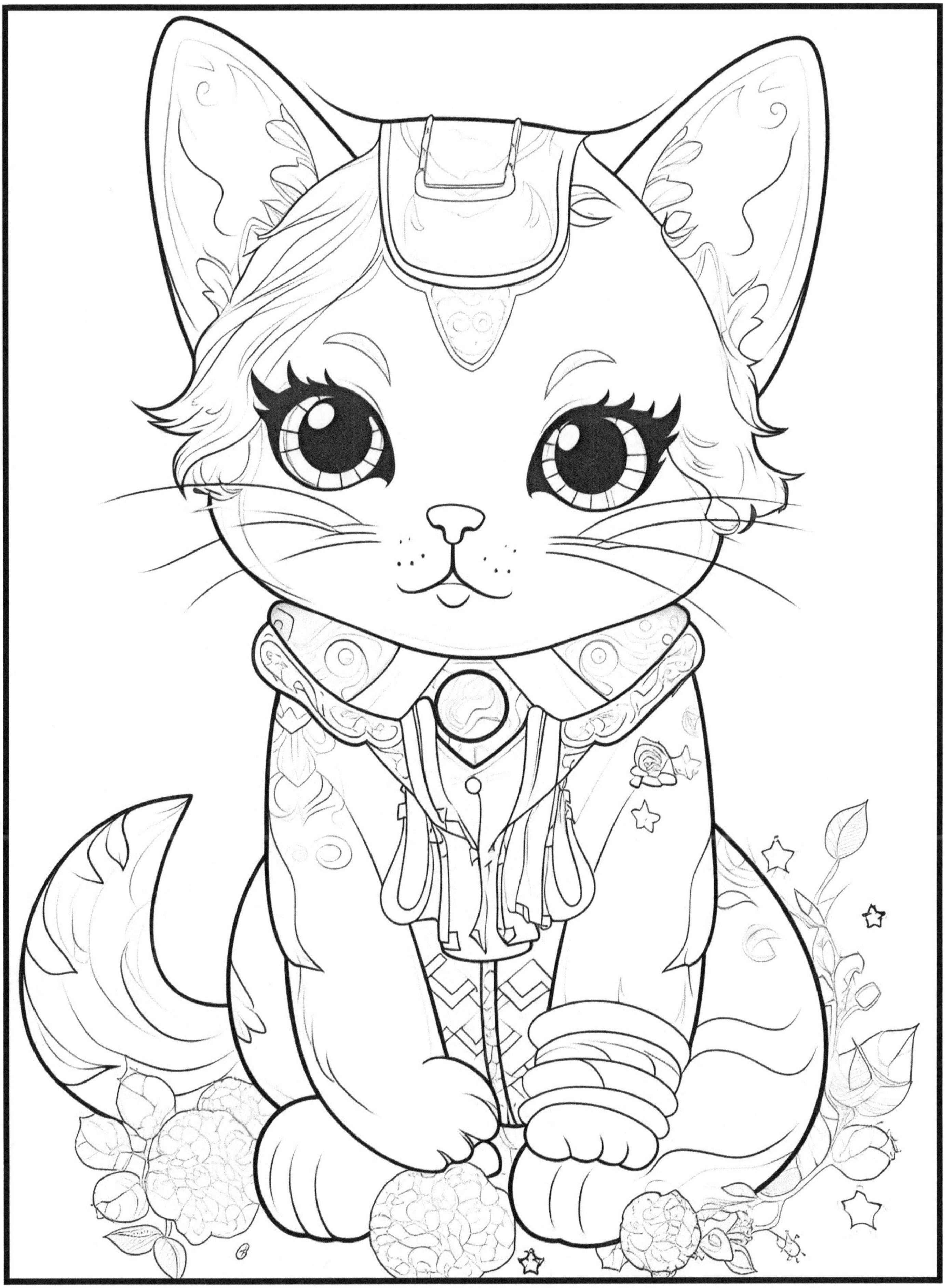

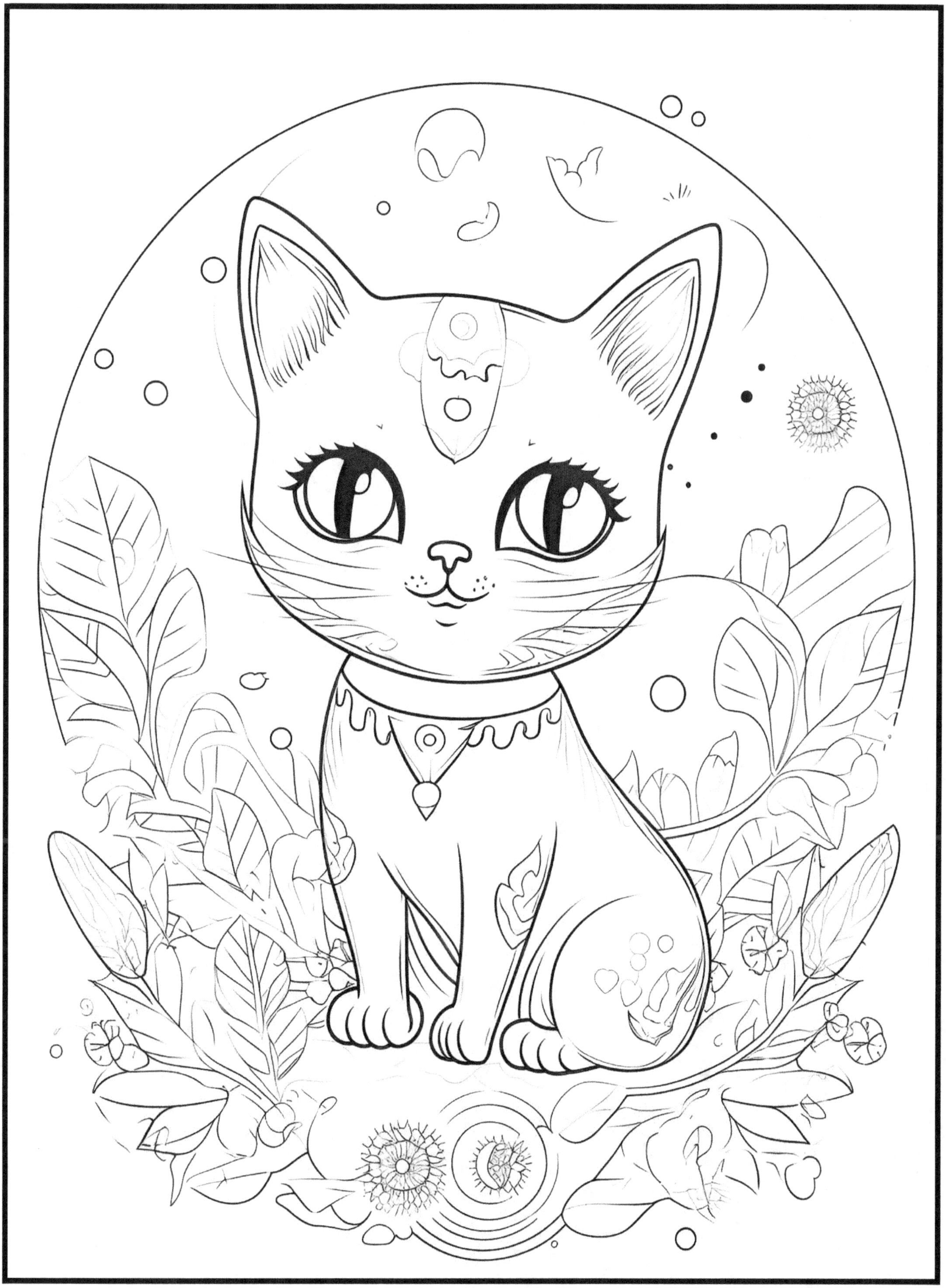

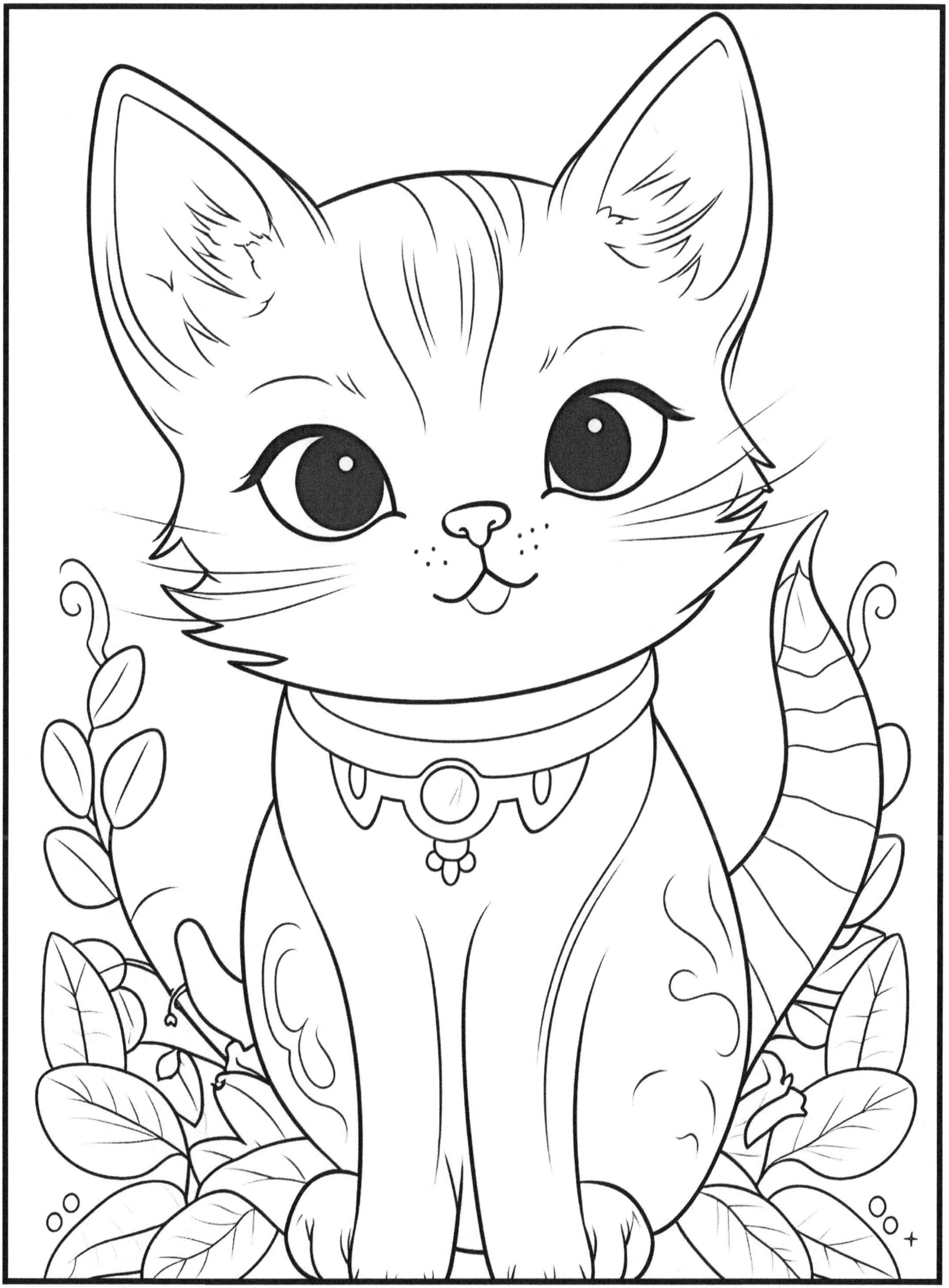

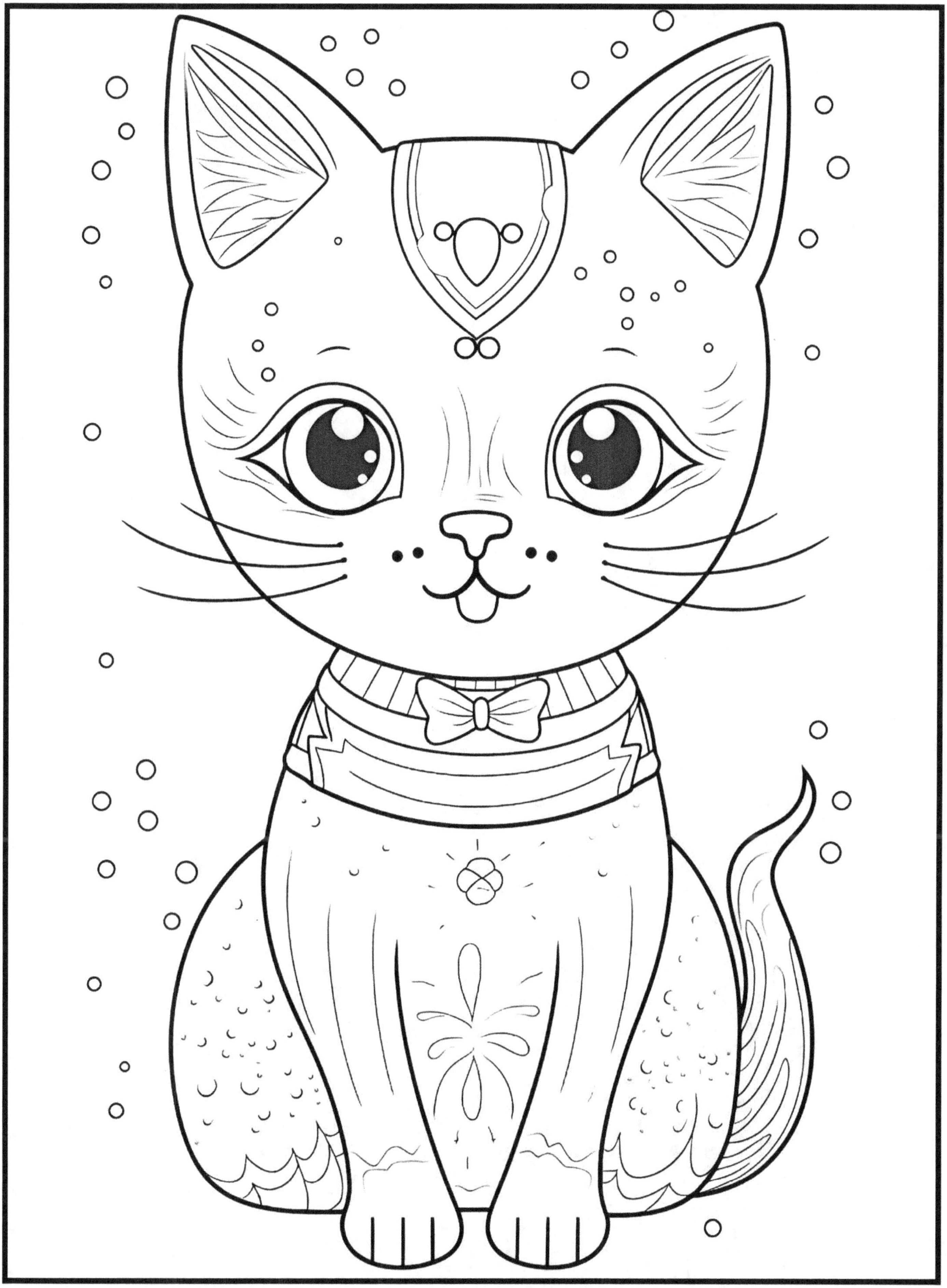

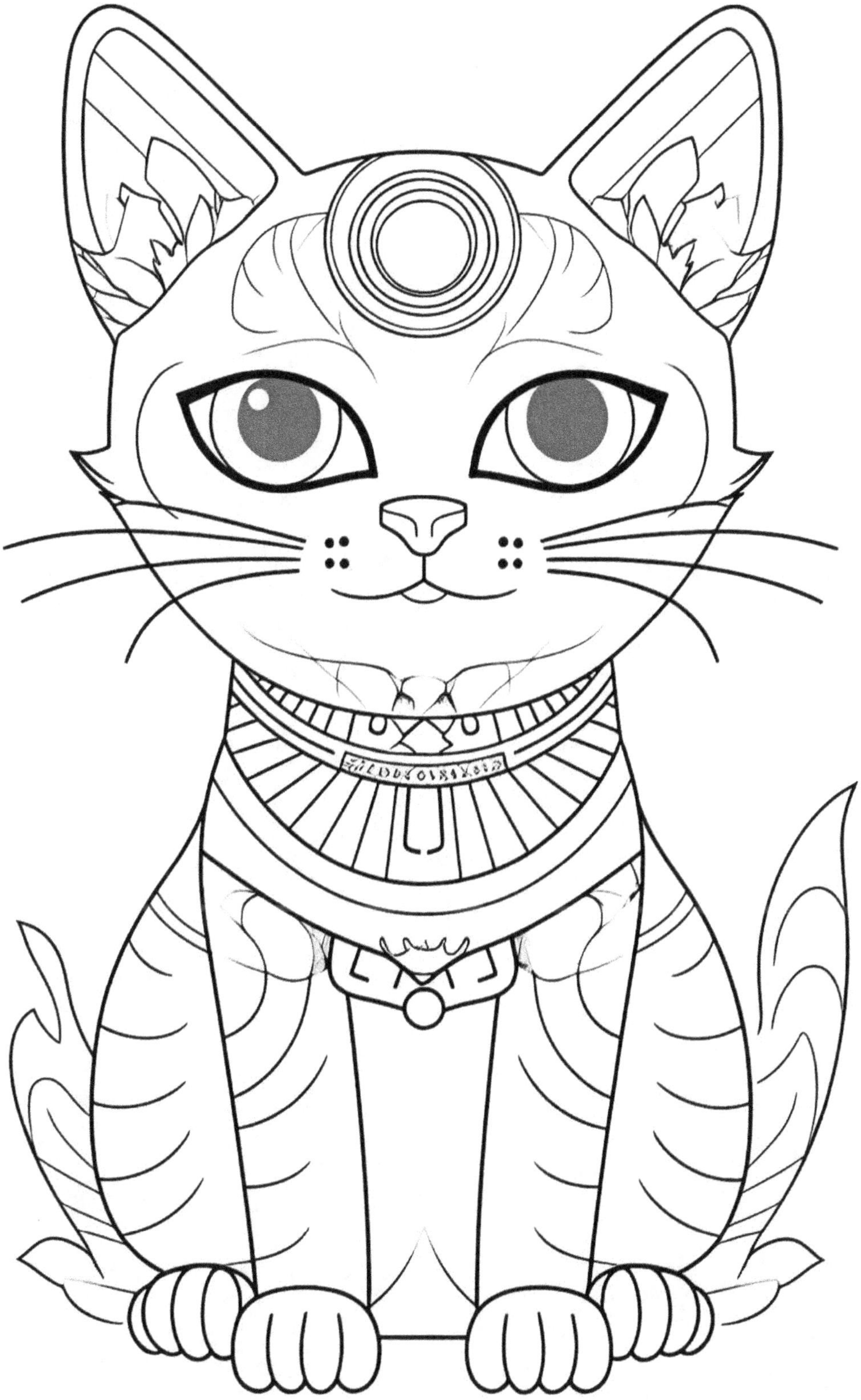

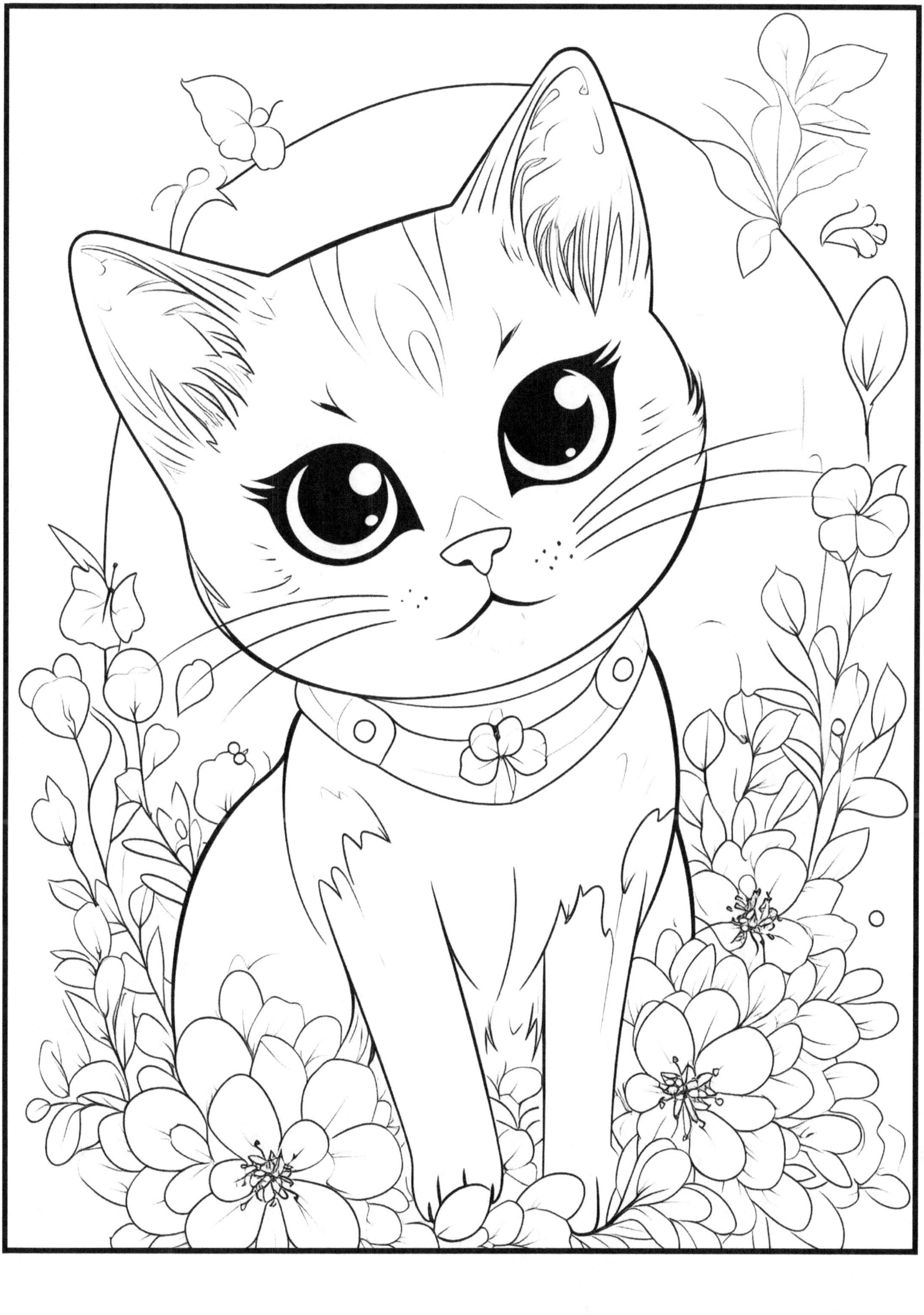

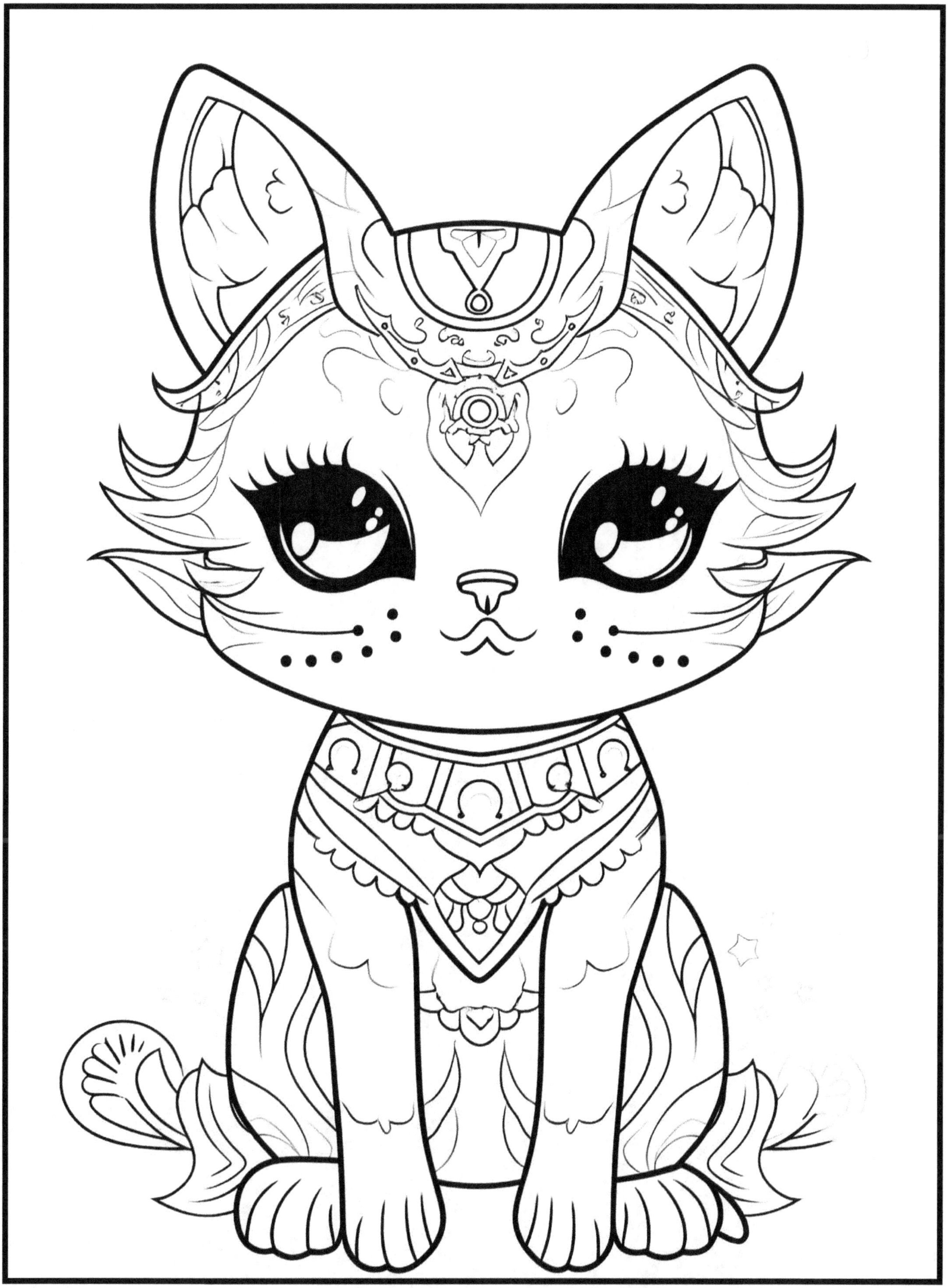

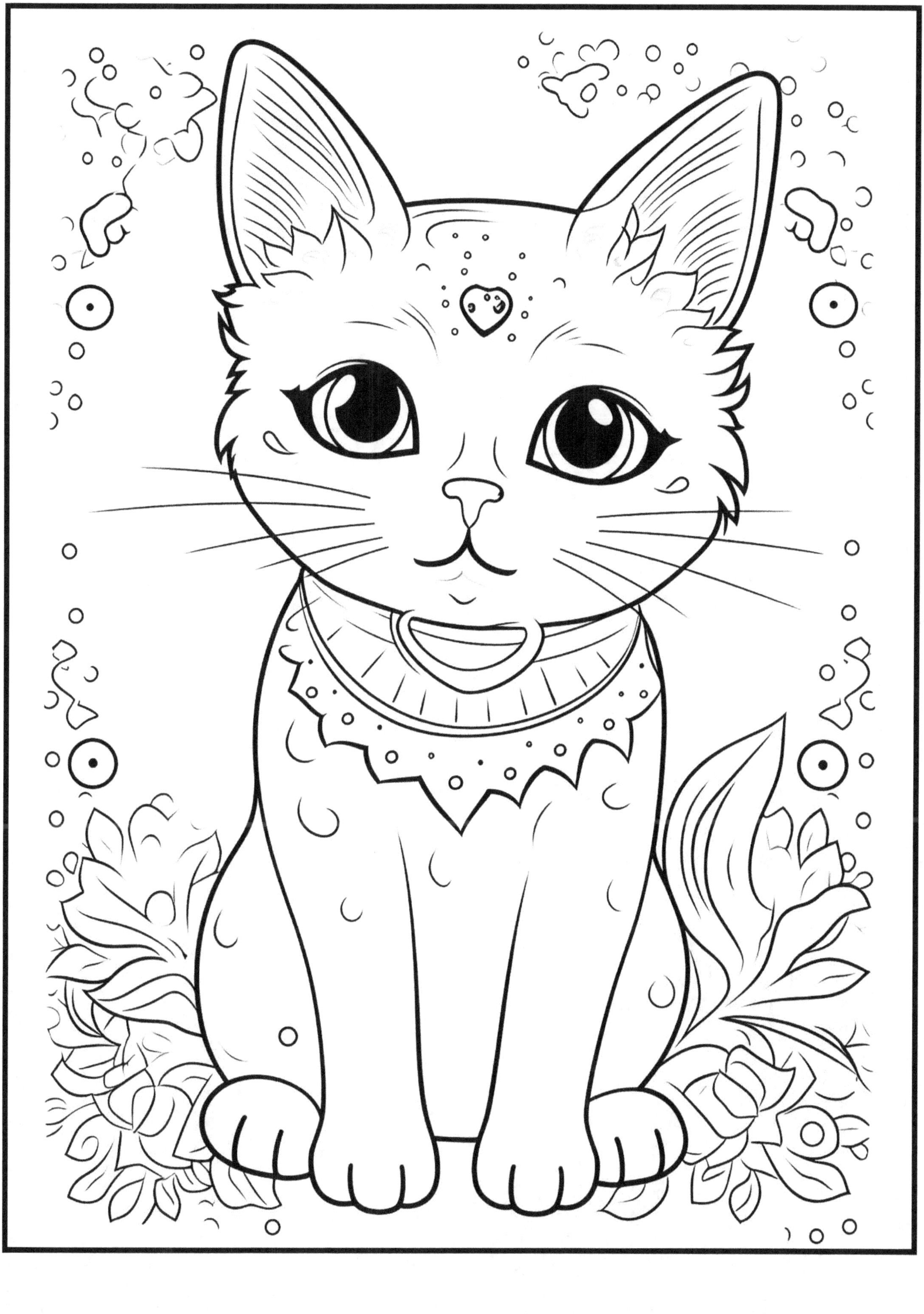

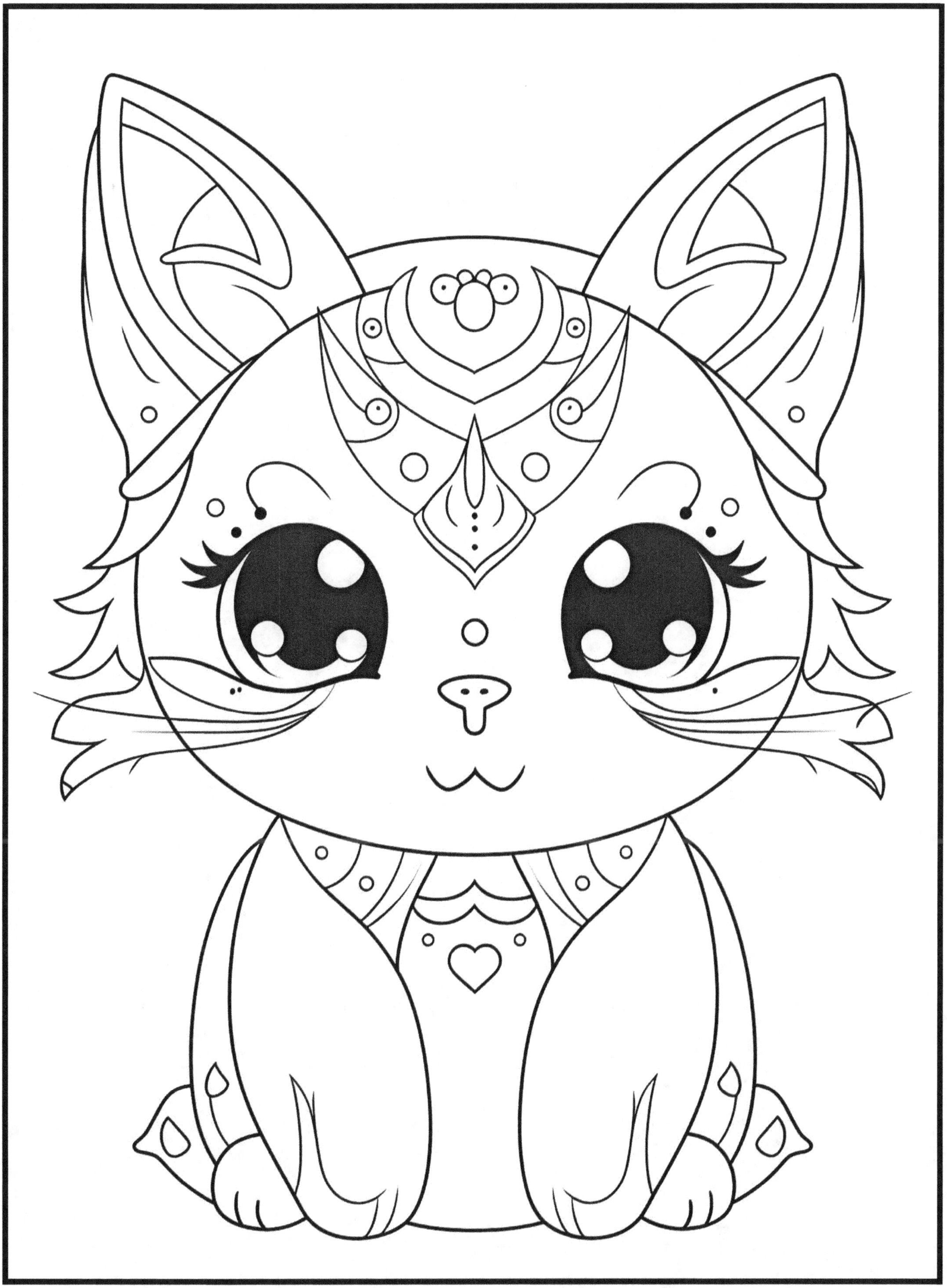

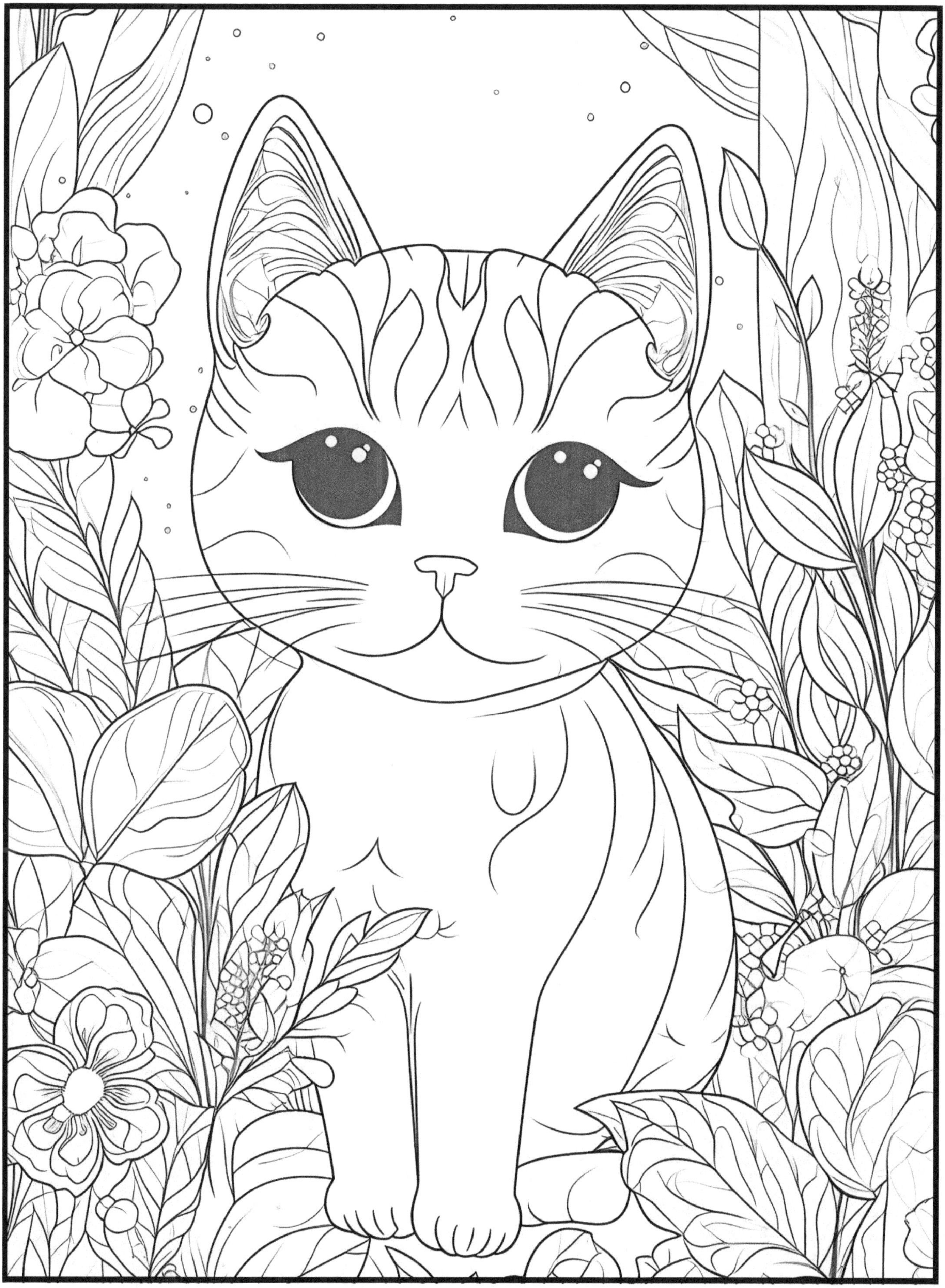

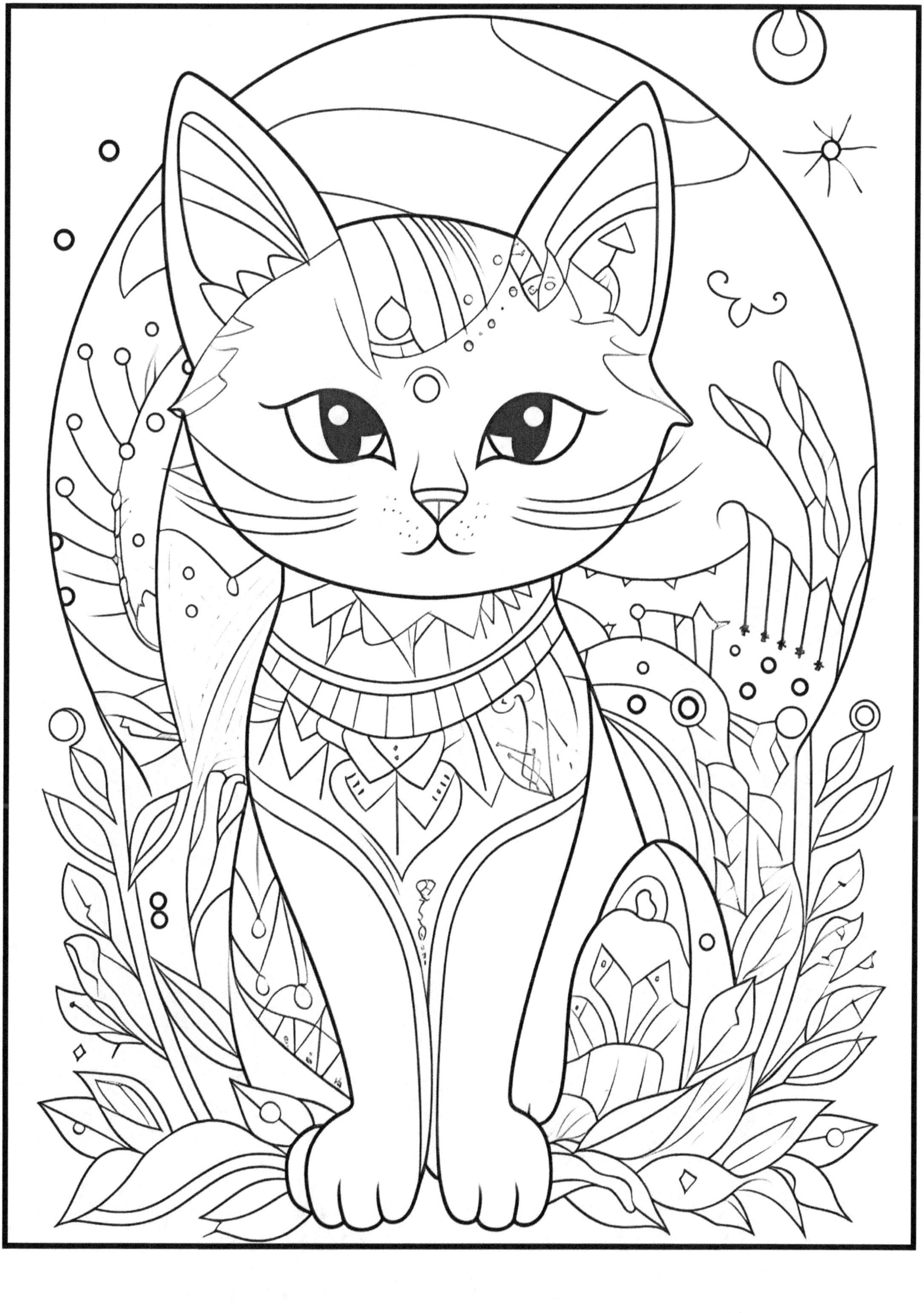

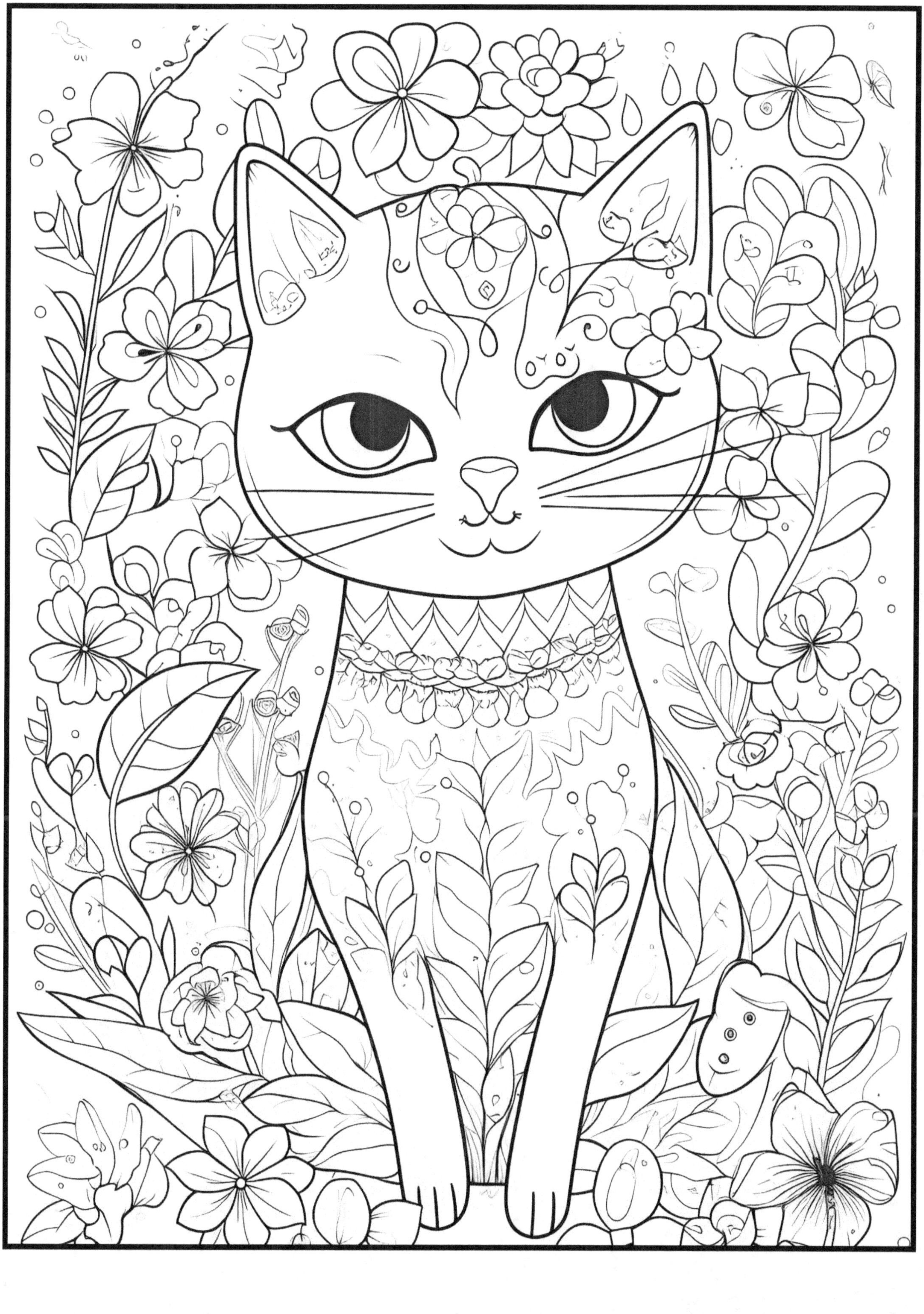

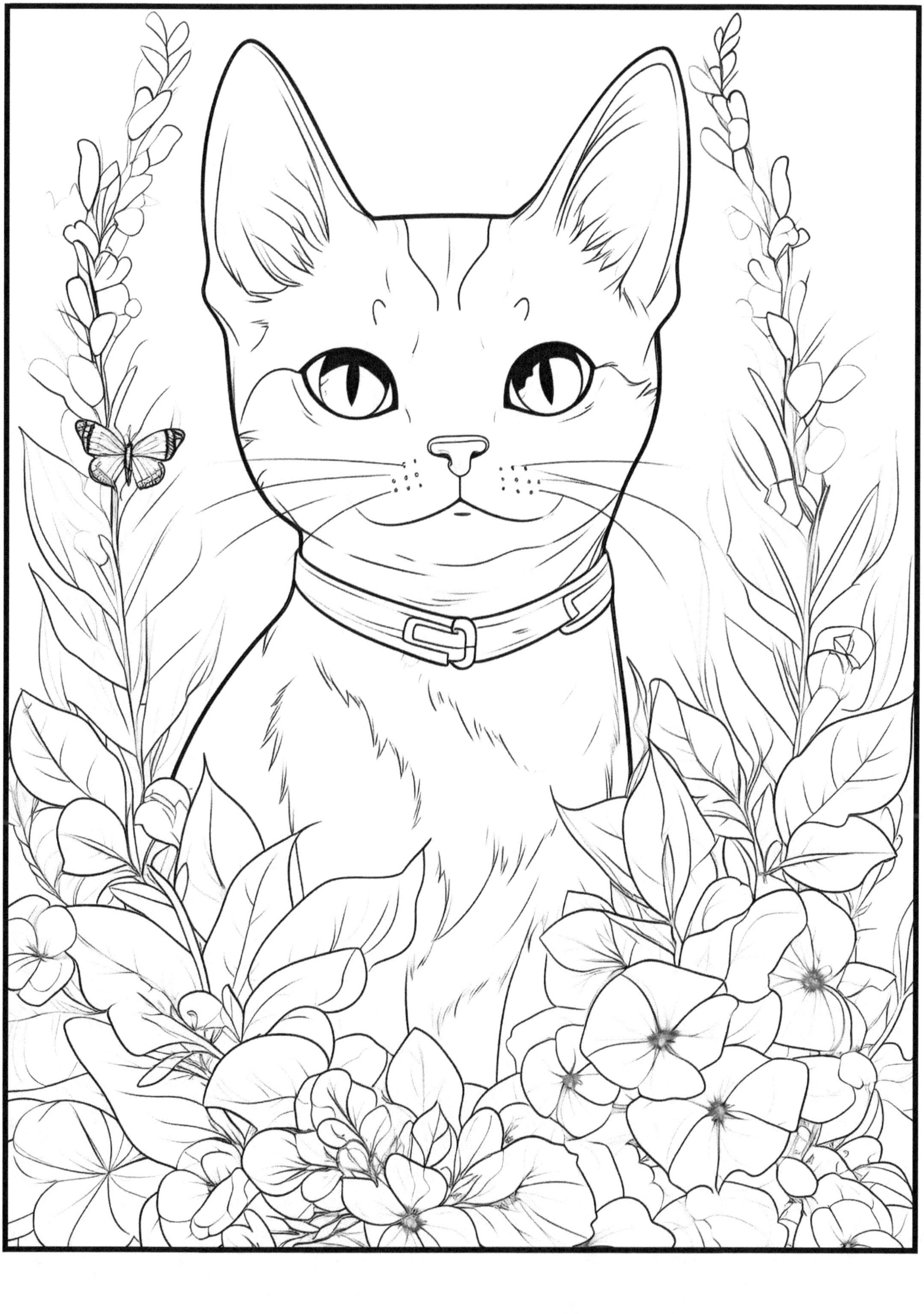

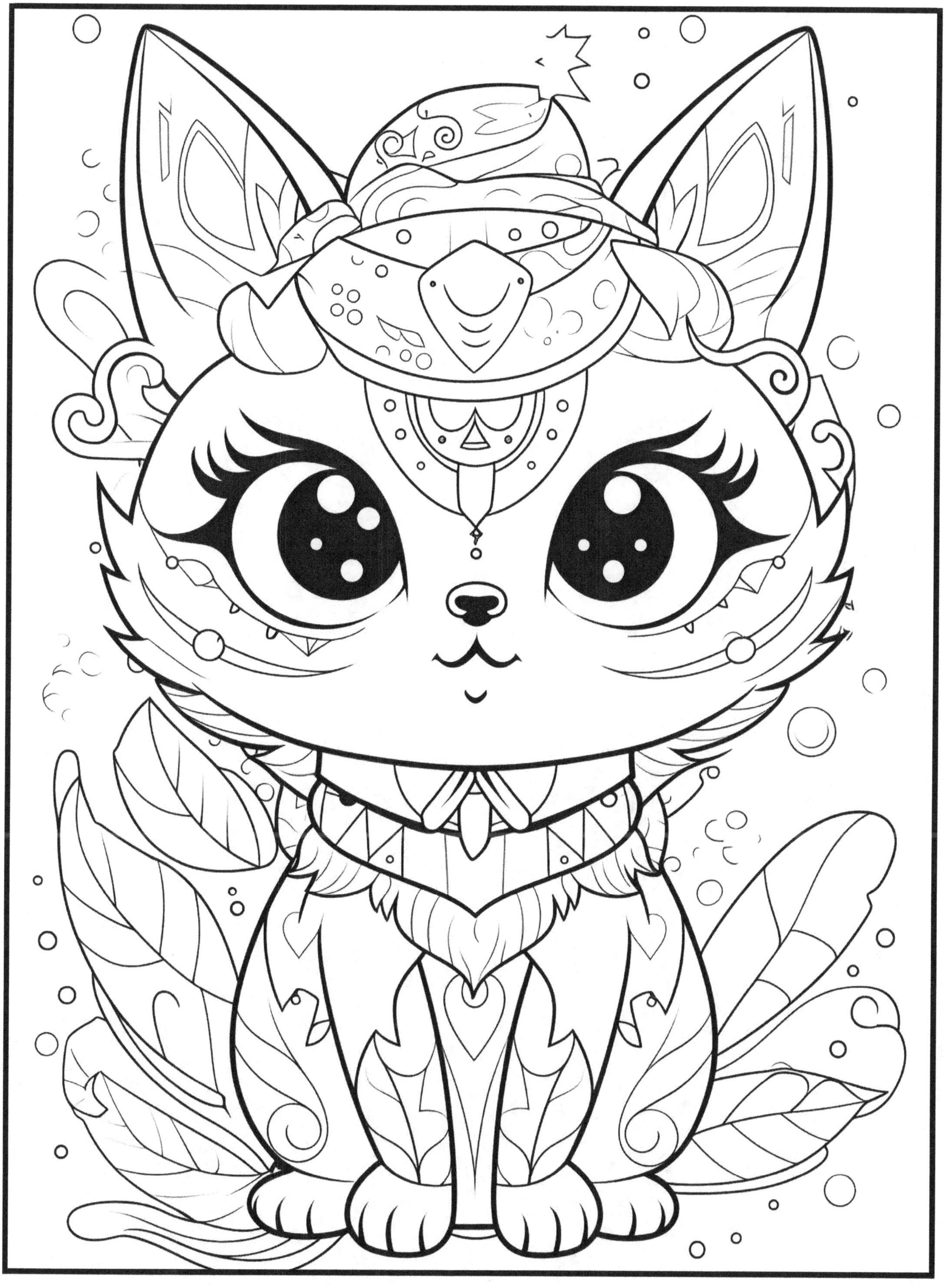

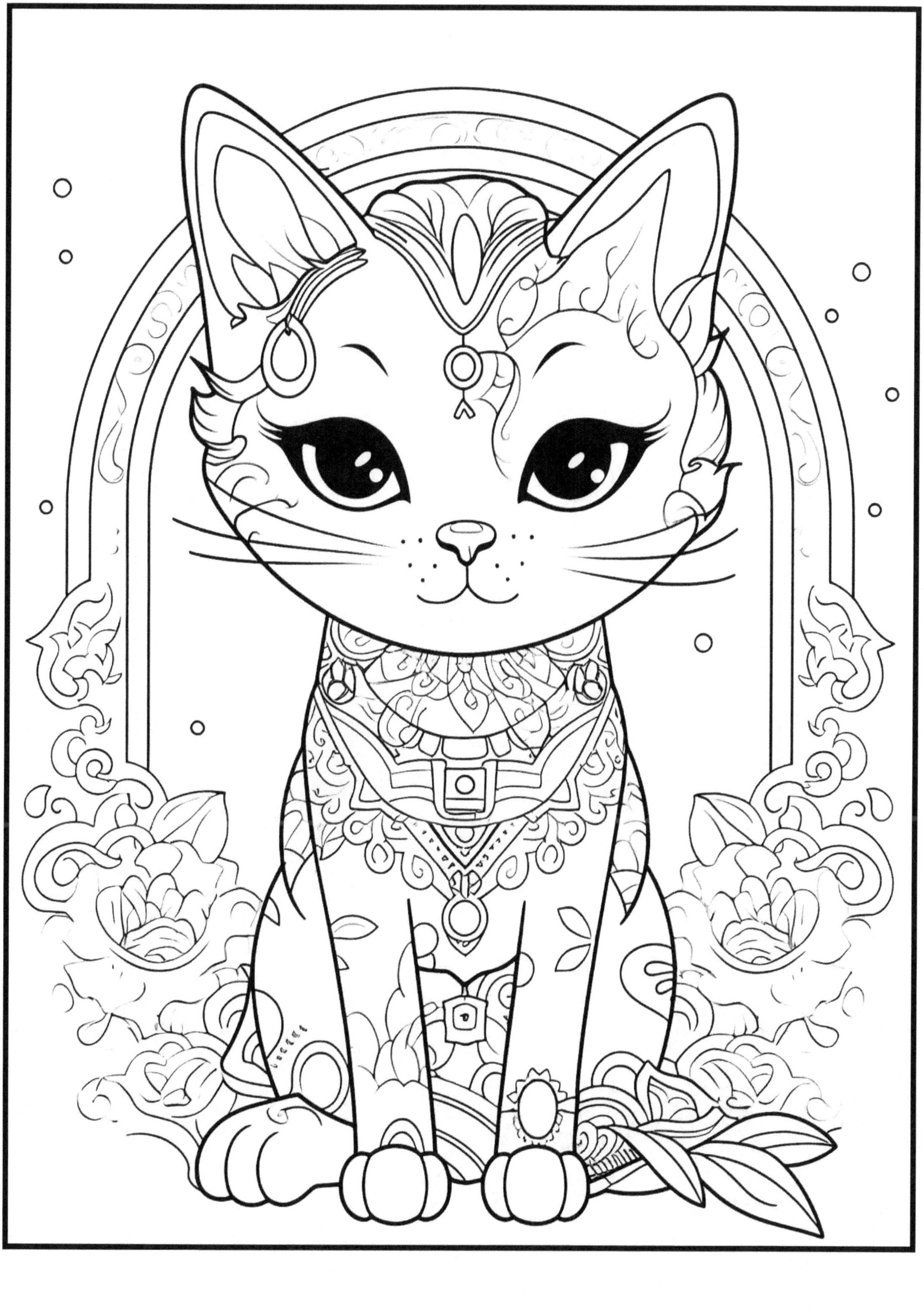

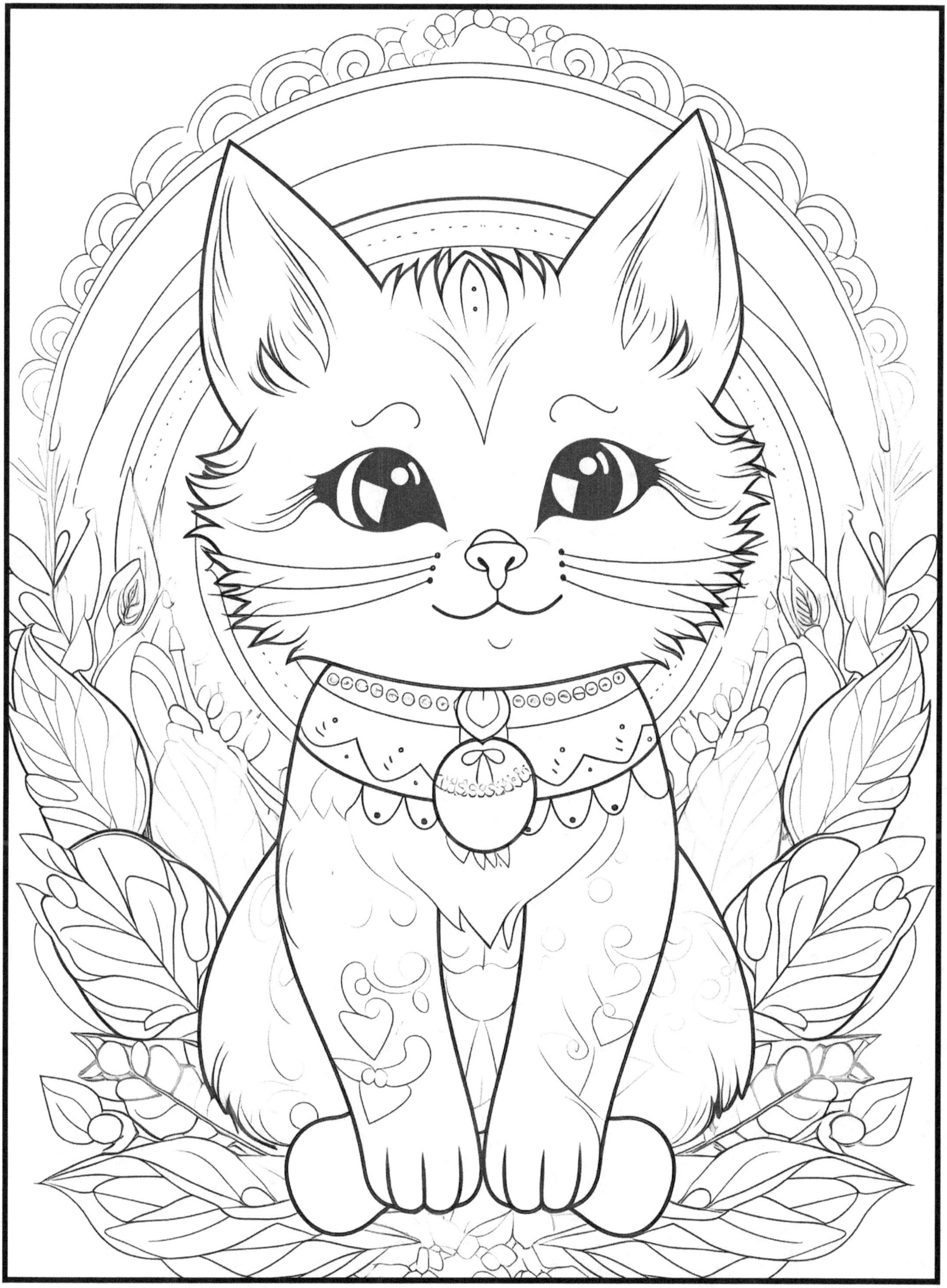

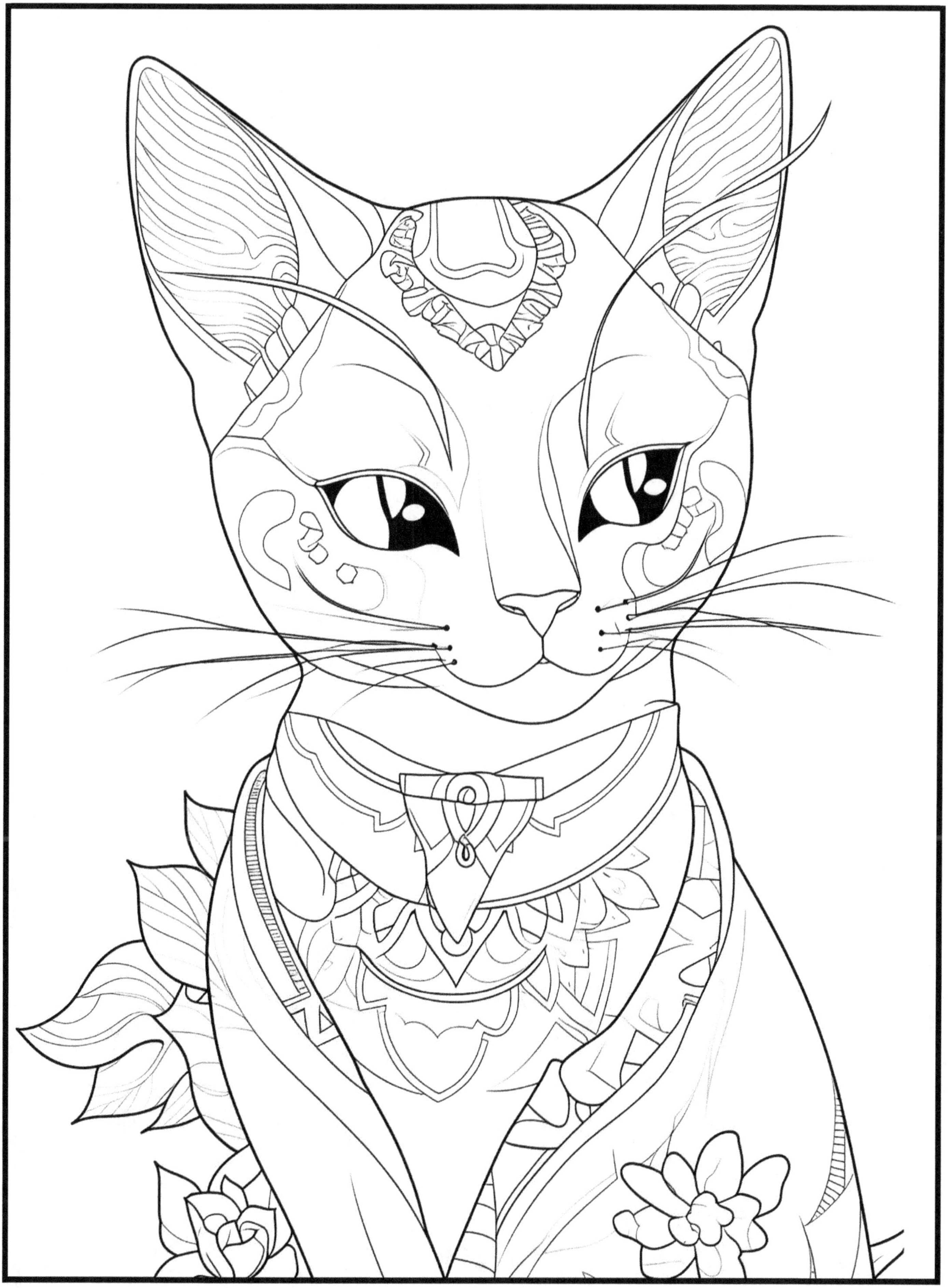

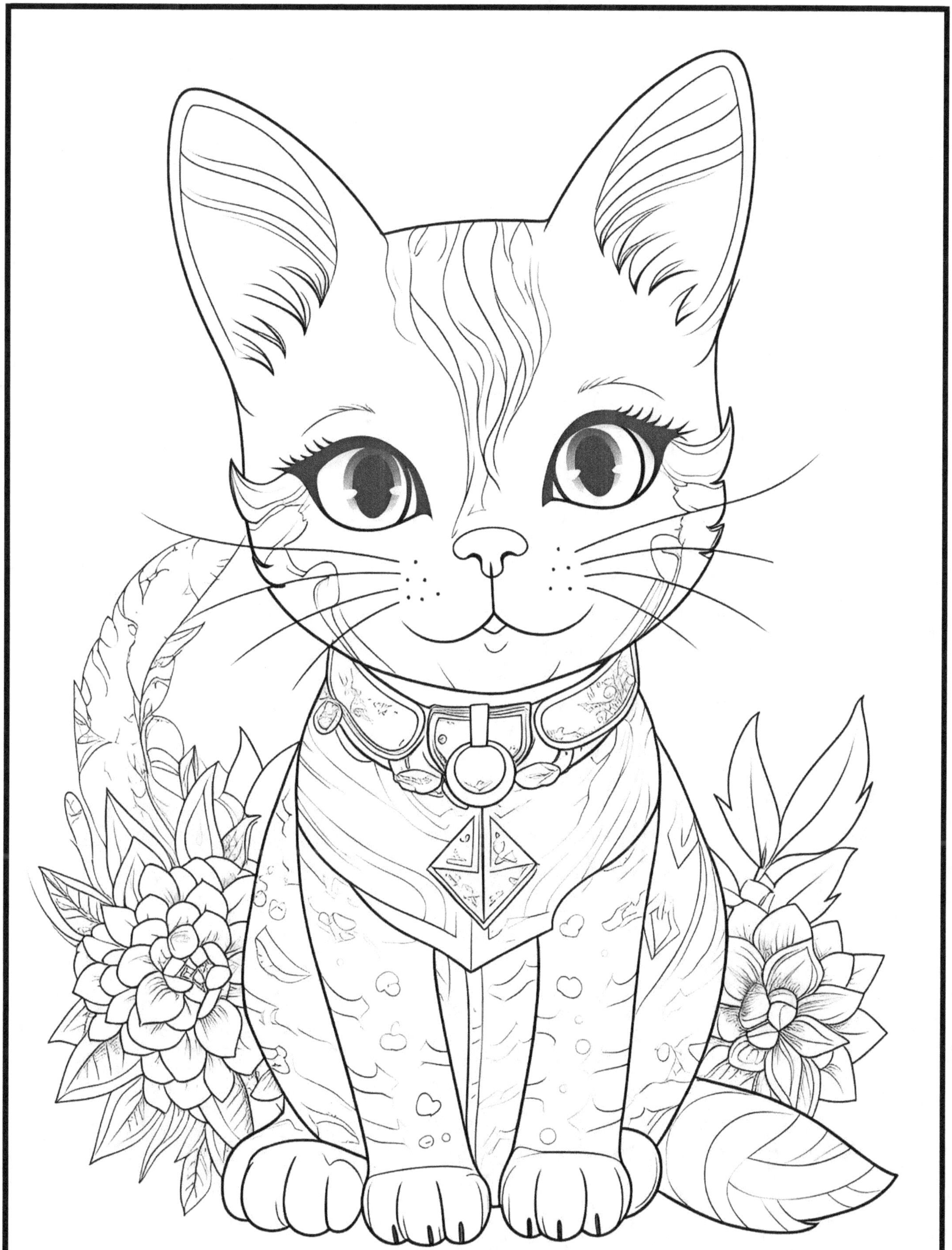

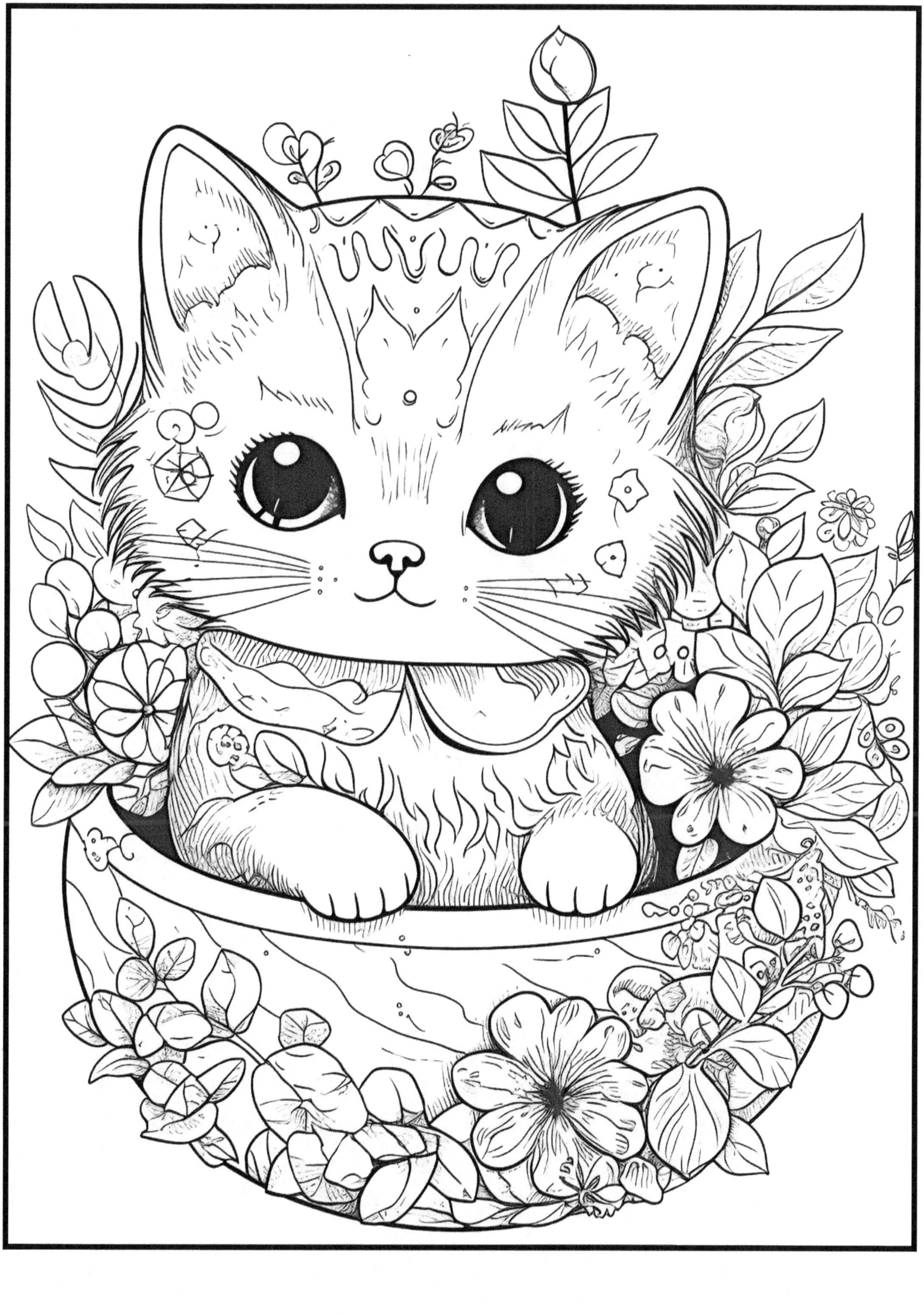

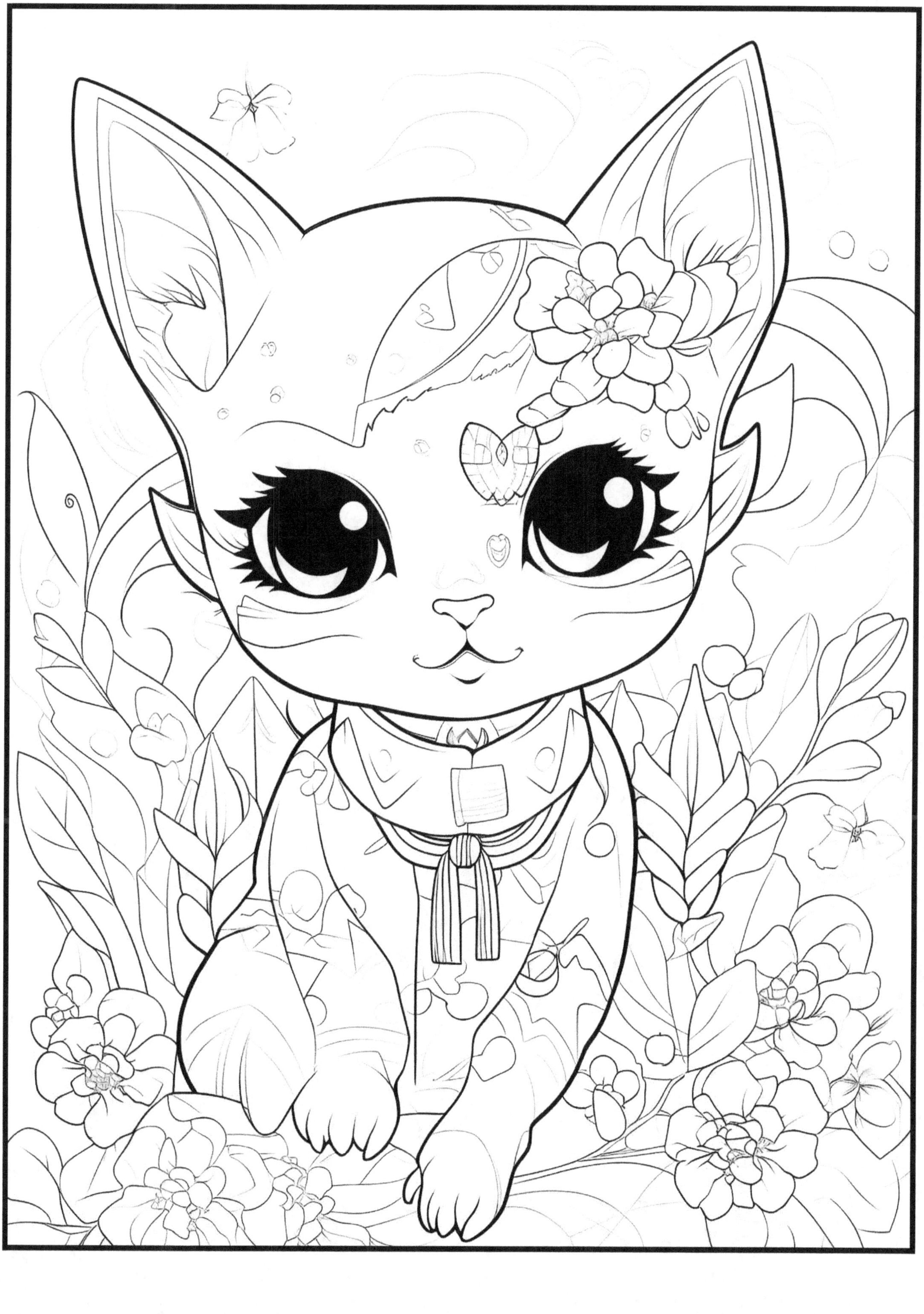

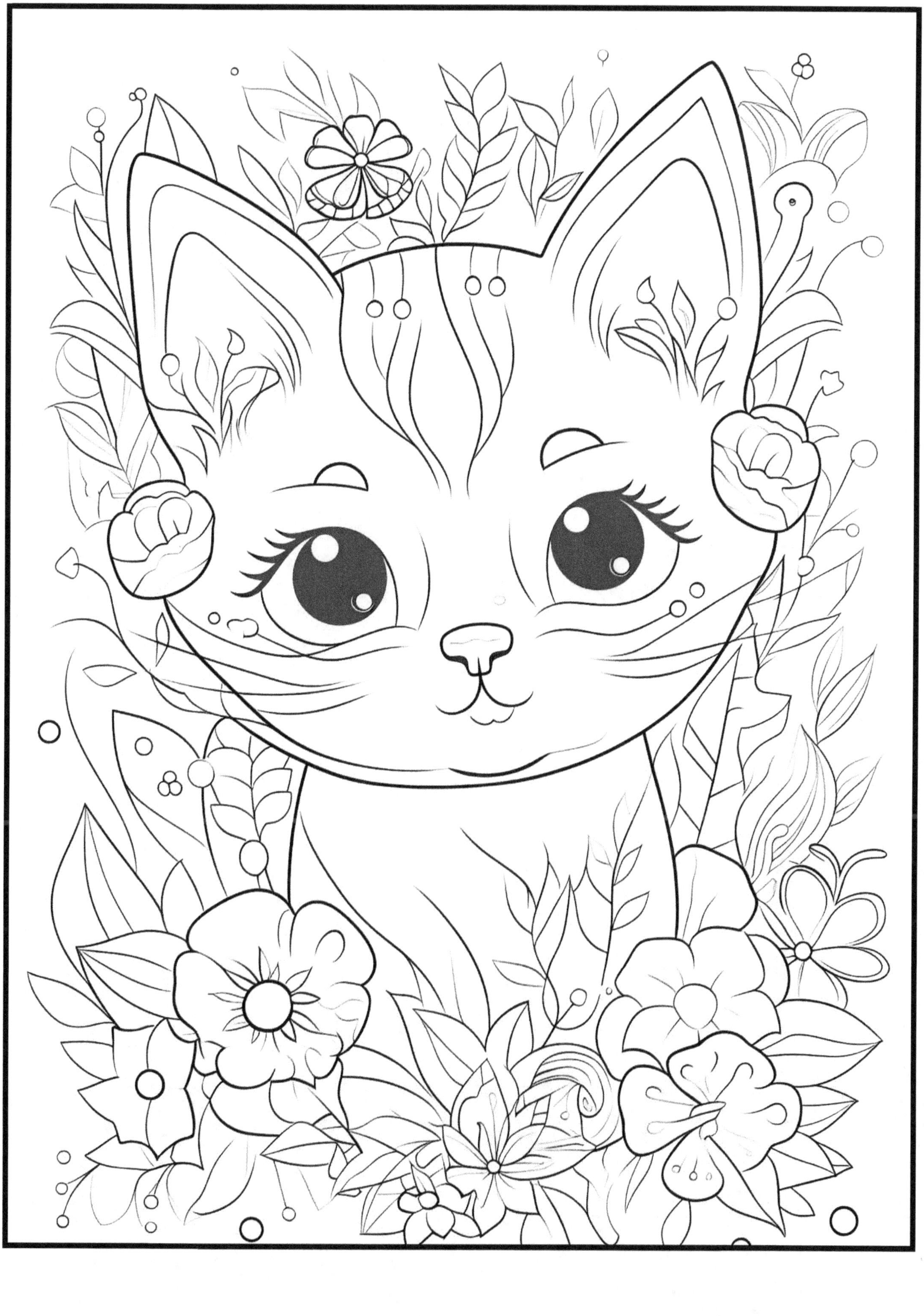

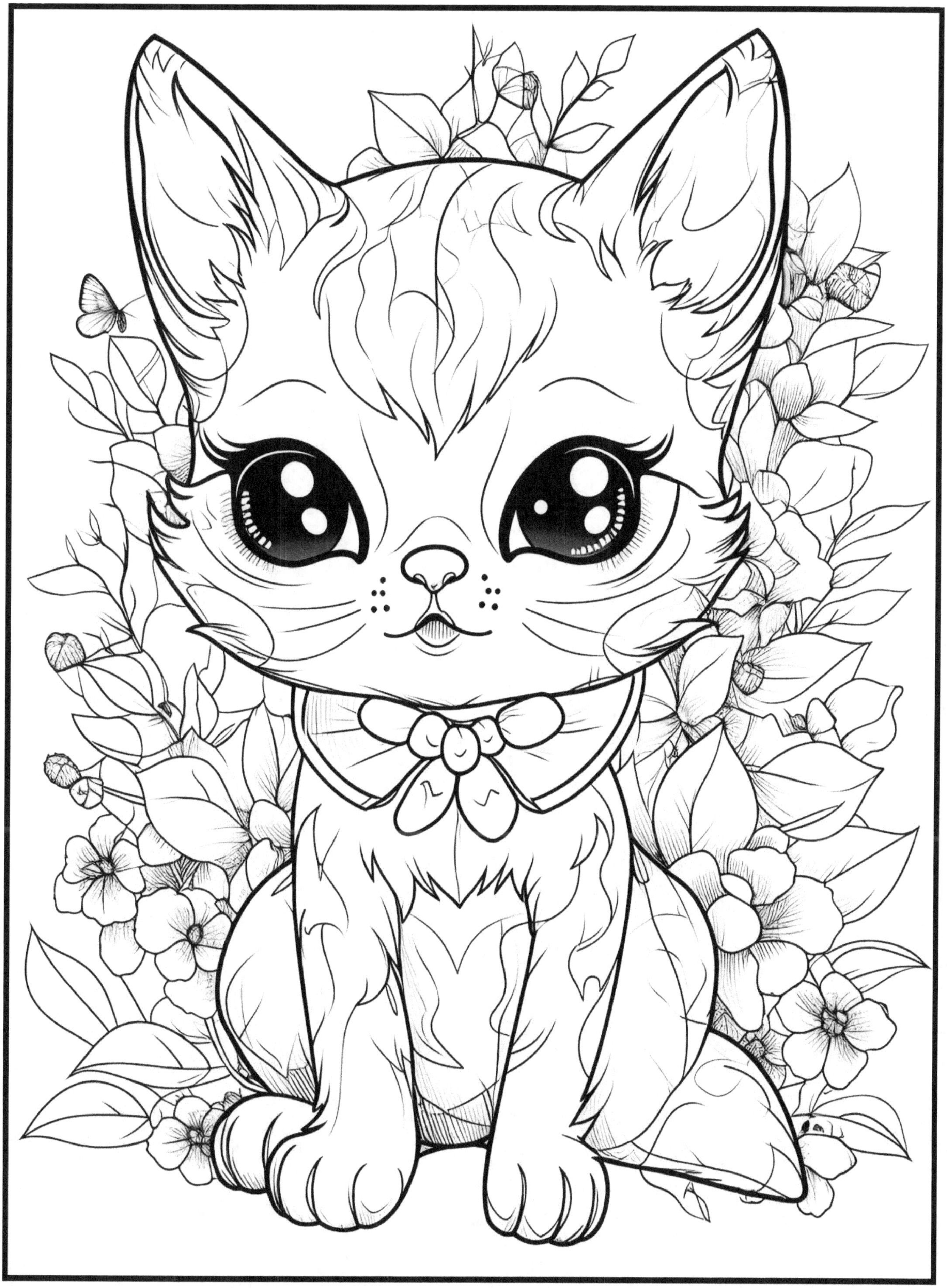

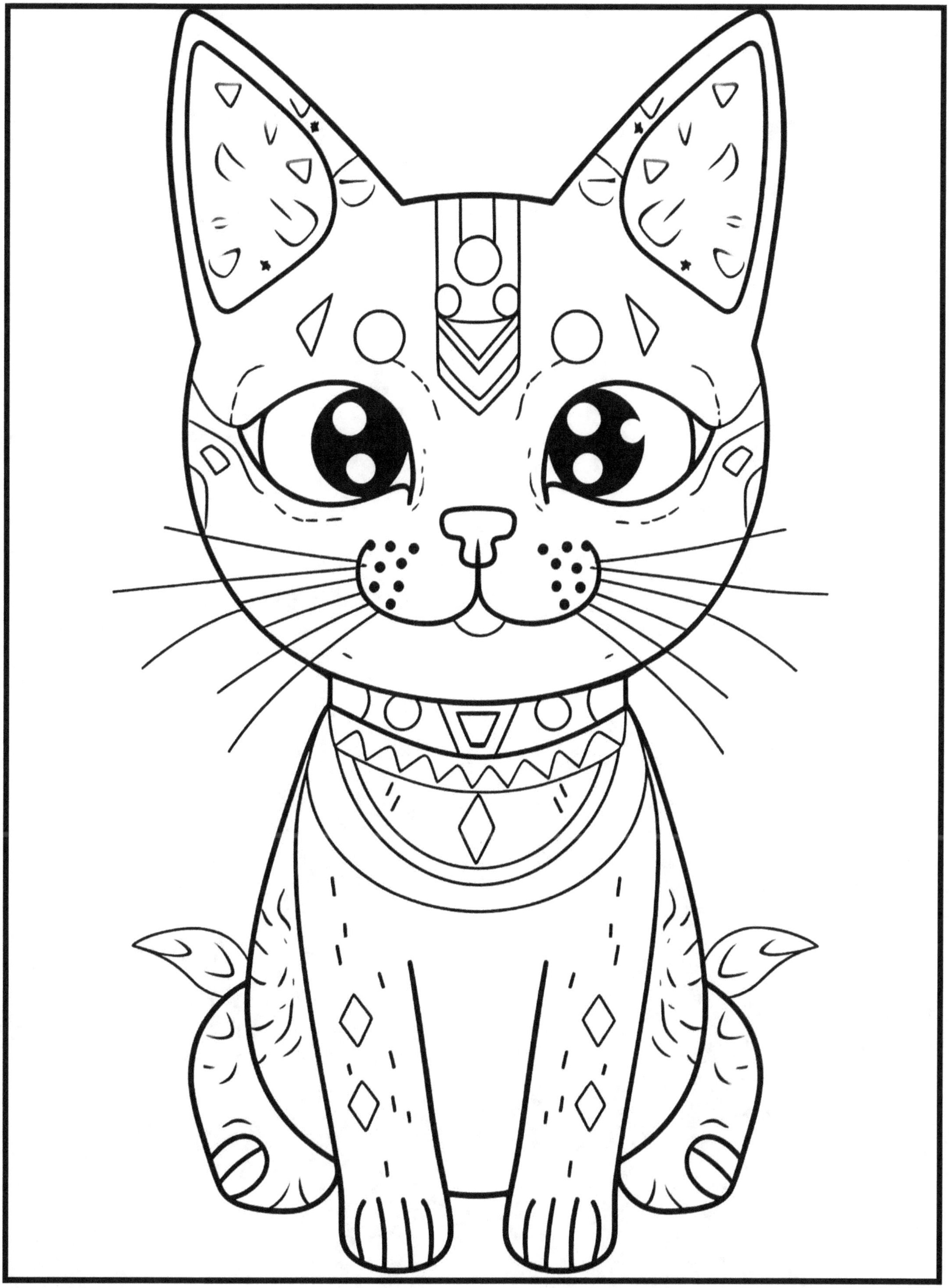

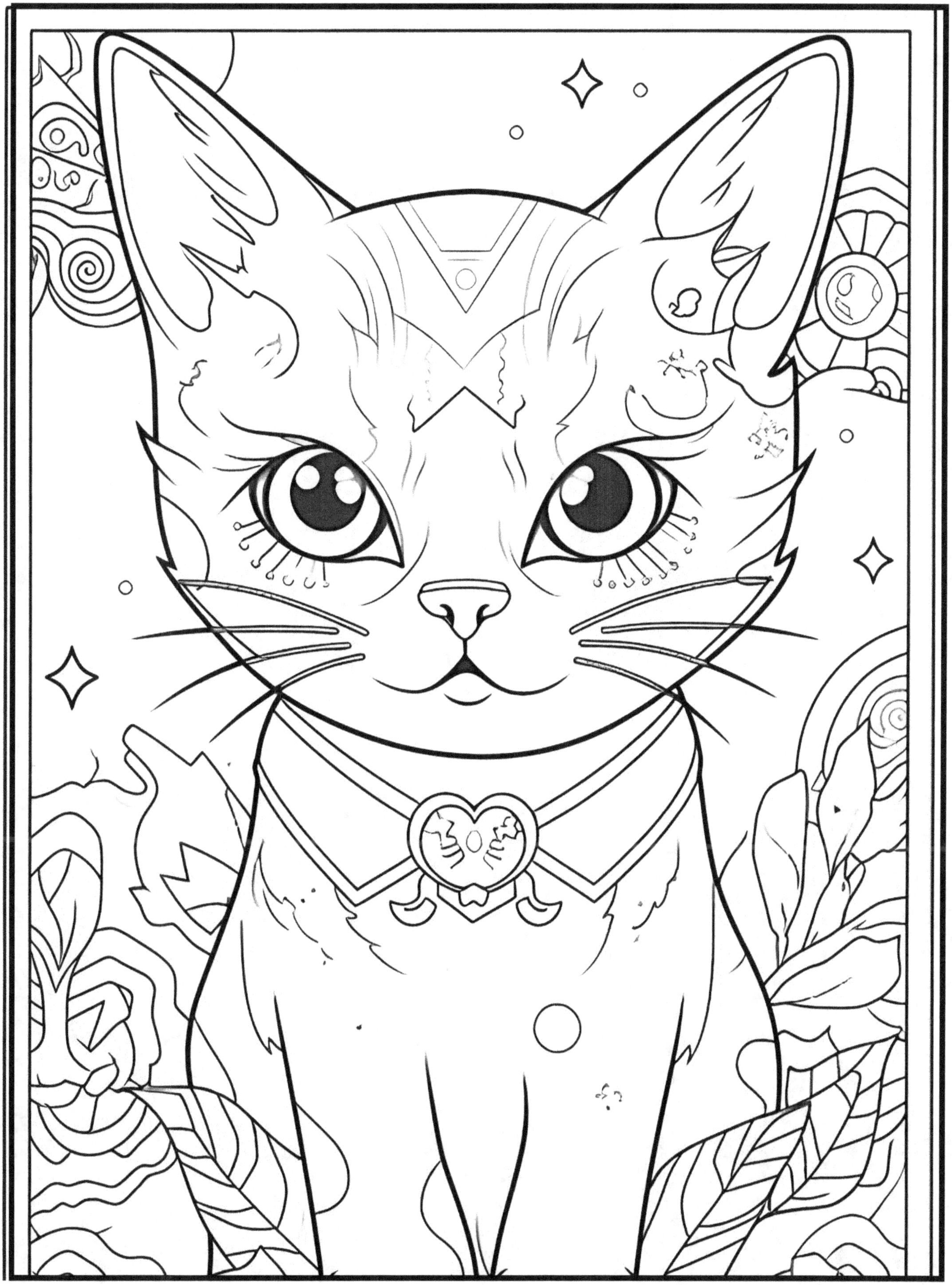

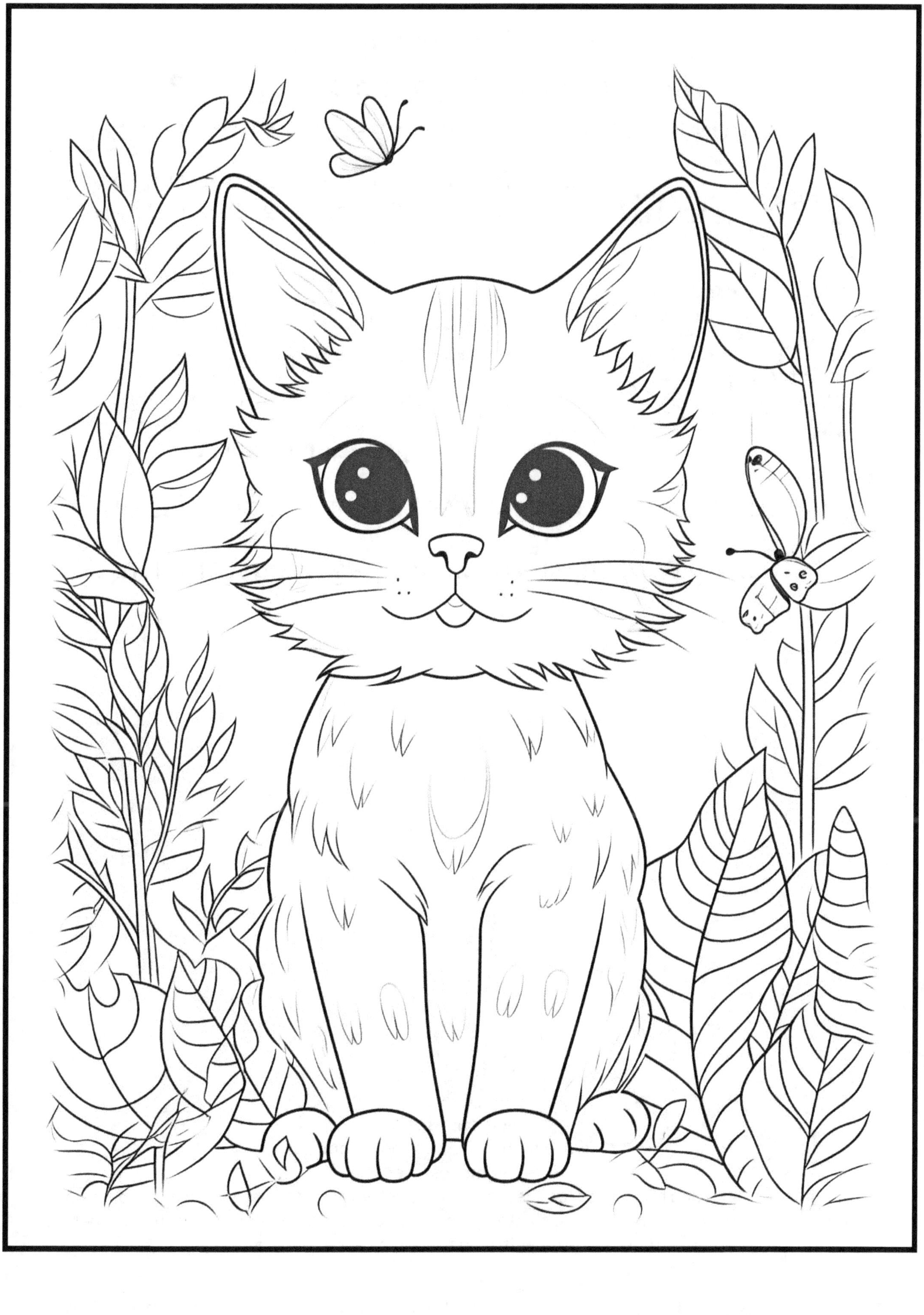

Love this Coloring book?
Want to show off your masterpiece?
Do you want your art displayed on our website?

1. Take a picture of a finished coloring page
2. Scan the QR Code to go to our website
3. Upload the photo of your finished coloring page

OR

Use #happytimesbooks or mention us @happytimesbooks on Instragram to have it displayed on our front page

No registration required

If you are under 18 please get a parents permission

https://happytimesbooks.com/pages/customer-art

Copyright
Charles King
Cute Cats: Vol 5

Self-published
charles@happytimesbooks.com

www.ingramcontent.com/pod-product-compliance
Lightning Source LLC
Chambersburg PA
CBHW080457030726
47592CB00011B/3149
9781961877153